In Chris Rattay's book, *Word* treasures. Chris takes us back to the basics of our faith of love, reconciliation, forgiveness, and following Jesus with all of our hearts. Chris has not only lived out each of these chapters in his personal life and relationships, but has helped so many others find freedom and joy by simply obeying and loving Jesus. It is what has always changed the world and always will. His words and his life are powerful and needed for all of us today.

Jimmy Siebert, Senior Pastor, Antioch Community Church, President, Antioch Ministries International

Long before Chris starting writing down his words, I watched him study God's Words. And walk by them. Over nearly 20 years, I've seen in Chris a particular sort of courage and integrity: one that's caused him to make decisions—about the gospel, about money, about justice, about where he was going to live and who he was going to associate with—which haven't always seemed popular at the time, seemed to bear fruit right away, and which have come at great cost to him (and his family). But he's stood strong and persevered. And the result is in his family. And the people he's ministered to. And here on these pages. They're words Chris has walked by, and as a result, they have a sense of reality that's good for the soul. And an antidote to our shallow, just-words world.

John Lo, Lead Pastor, Epicentre Church

If you've had your fill of empty platitudes, hollow sermons, and out-of-touch preachers whose words say more than their lives, Chris Rattay is the leader you're looking for. Chris's life is the heart of his message; he doesn't say a word about God that he hasn't already lived out with his whole family and community. Your journey through this book will be one of sitting at the feet of a man who has put Jesus' words into practice, and who has the joys, the scars, the faith, and the failures to prove it. You're not about to read ideas about Jesus, you're about to read a challenge to life with Jesus.

Scott Hall, Associate Director of Urban Programs,
InterVarsity Christian Fellowship

Discipleship is messy, but it's where people best heal and grow and experience life change. Chris and his wife Maggie are disciples of Jesus who make disciples. In Chris' new book, *Words to Walk By*, he has provided a proven model with solid content for helping Christ followers to more intentionally go and make disciples as well. Don't get it twisted: discipleship is the assignment, and this valuable resource will help you fulfill it in community with those around you!

Dr. Larry Acosta, Founder/CEO,
Urban Youth Workers Institute

This book so clearly illustrates that obedience to Jesus brings life. Chris Rattay lays out the many ways we avoid grappling with our sinfulness at the expense of the transformation God offers us. This is not an abstract, theological reflection on Jesus' Sermon on the Mount. It is first and foremost a practical manual for how to live into it, which, as Rattay rightly argues, is the most crucial element. He calls us to break out of our spiritual complacency to rediscover Jesus' lordship. But the best part of his reflections are the stories that prove that those who seek to live out Jesus' teaching will be liberated into true life. What he writes is not always comfortable to hear, but the words of life rarely are.

Derek W. Engdahl, Co-General Director,
Servant Partners

We all long to see transformation in peoples' lives, including our own. What does this actually look like on our streets and where we live our lives? Chris Rattay weaves together stories from years of life in East LA with principles from the Sermon on the Mount to show us how deep discipleship leads to the lasting transformation. A clearly written, insightful, and compelling guide that will help those who truly want to follow Jesus, and guide others on the way.

Jude Tiersma Watson, InnerChange/CRM,
Associate Professor of Urban Mission, Fuller Seminary

Chris Rattay has impacted me deeply both through his lifestyle and his teaching. I am so thankful that he has written a book on discipleship so a larger audience can learn from him. As I read Chris' new book, I was convicted by his humility and authenticity and was inspired to freshly apply Jesus' words to my life.

Robert Herber, Lead Pastor,
All Peoples Church, San Diego

Words to Walk By offers profound theology, compelling stories, and practical insights for urban disciples. Chris Rattay's depth in the Word and two decades of ministry experience are evident on every page. This book is an important resource for small groups and churches of all sizes, especially those in multiethnic and multi-class settings.

Dr. John Teter, Senior Pastor, Fountain of Life
Covenant Church, Executive Director, FOL Antioch

Chris Rattay brings us a gritty and honest look at Jesus' sermon on the mount. He first and foremost holds himself to Jesus' teaching. Then he applies it to us. His stories are inspiring and practical, seeped in his urban ministry experiences. Enjoy!

Doug Schaupp, Associate National Director,
Evangelism, InterVarsity Christian Fellowship/USA

WORDS TO
WALK BY

WORDS TO WALK BY

A DISCIPLESHIP GUIDE THROUGH
THE SERMON ON THE MOUNT

CHRIS RATTAY

SERVANT PARTNERS PRESS

Words to Walk By: A Discipleship Guide Through the Sermon on the Mount. Copyright © 2016 by
Chris Rattay. All rights reserved.
Servant Partners Press
P.O. Box 3144
Pomona, CA 91769
www.servantpartnerspress.org and *www.servantpartners.org*

No part of this publication may be reproduced, stored in, or introduced
into a retrieval system, or transmitted, in any form, or by any means
(electronic, mechanical, photocopying, recording, or otherwise), without
the prior written permission of the publisher. Requests for submission
should be directed to *permissions@servantpartnerspress.org,* or mailed
to Permissions, Servant Partners Press, P.O. Box 3144, Pomona, CA 91769.

Servant Partners is an interdenominational evangelical missions agency
that sends, trains, and equips those who follow Jesus by living among
the world's urban poor. By the power of the Holy Spirit, we seek the
transformation of communities with the urban poor through church
planting, community organizing, and leadership development.

Cover Art provided by Bob (Uncle Bacon) Hurton
Cover and Book design:
Loren A. Roberts/HearkenCreative (*hearkencreative.com*)

Scriptures taken from the Holy Bible, New International Version®, NIV®.
Copyright © 1973, 1978, 1984, 2011 by Biblica, Inc.™ Used by permission of
Zondervan. All rights reserved worldwide. www.zondervan.com The "NIV"
and "New International Version" are trademarks registered in the United
States Patent and Trademark Office by Biblica, Inc.™

print ISBN: 978-0-9983665-2-4 (ISBN 13)

CONTENTS

ACKNOWLEDGEMENTS

I AM SO GRATEFUL to the team of people God has put around me, who have taught and shown me what it means to be a disciple of Jesus. There is no such thing as a self-made person, as none of us grow up in a vacuum. I am supported by amazing parents, incredible relatives, and a vibrant spiritual family. I am so thankful to Ken Zell, Derek and Lisa Engdahl, John Lo, Jonny Eveleth, Ricky Ramirez, Scott and Jenny Hall, John Teter, Jen Lee, Kevin Rhodes, Jen and Jon Ball, Robert Herber, my entire New Life Community family, and the team at Servant Partners Press.

Every one of you has shown me a part of the Sermon on the Mount, a unique aspect of being Jesus' disciple. My highest gratitude goes to my wife and kids. Maggie, Josiah, Jaden, and Sami, you are the greatest gifts God has given me! I am so amazed at your love for Jesus and your courage to live out the Sermon on the Mount with me. You inspire me to keep trusting Jesus. I love you!

This book has been shaped by all of the people mentioned above; it has also been shaped by books. There is nothing written that is original, save for the words of Jesus, and my book is no exception. As you read, you will find J.C. Ryle, Martyn Lloyd Jones, Dietrich Bonhoeffer, and Dallas Willard walking through these pages, and though I might not be able to fill their shoes, I'm glad to be able to at least walk the path of discipleship with them.

A JOURNEY OF TRANSFORMATION

IN CHAPTER 4 OF THE Gospel of Matthew, Jesus starts His public ministry with fireworks, as He defeats the devil in a three-round desert smackdown. After He makes it clear that He is the shot-caller, He enters into His hometown of Galilee and begins healing the sick from every illness and casting out demons. Revival is beginning! There is excitement in the air, crowds are beginning to form, and power is experienced. The kingdom of heaven is exploding onto earth. However, as soon as the crowds begin to form, Jesus does a most interesting thing: He sits everyone down and offers them discipleship. He calls people to be close to Him and follow Him in the long, difficult transformation of every part of their lives. Before the revival even gets off the ground, Jesus makes it very clear that His priority is the long, deep work of transformation. He refuses to be made into a celebrity preacher or a quick-fix guru.

Jesus guides us toward this transformation with the greatest sermon ever given. His first words speak directly to our warped mindset: "Blessed are the poor in spirit, for theirs is the kingdom of heaven." The kingdom of heaven can be ours right now, this same kingdom that defeated the devil and where the sick are healed. But it is a kingdom which is far from the confident, the gifted, and the successful. It is found instead among and within those poor in spirit. It is found in those who are hungry for new life, for transformation. And as we will see, it is found in those who hunger to obey Jesus rather than simply to see His power without any kind of trusting relationship. When we work to transform our hearts as Jesus calls us to do in the Sermon on the Mount, we find that life with Jesus is so much more than we could have imagined.

For the past ten years, I have lived and worked in East Los Angeles, a traditional hub for immigrants from Mexico and Central America. After a year of deepening our understanding of God's heart in the areas of racial and class reconciliation, my wife and I heard God call us to relocate to East LA. I knew that God was sending us to a neighborhood very different from our own, to both receive from the immigrant and Chicano community the character of God they uniquely carry, and to offer the character of God that we uniquely carry. Since East LA does not have a large percentage of people with post-high school education, and since it is a poor, working class community, it has sadly been stereotyped as a community that can only receive help. Yet, as we look at the totality of our Bible we realize that whether we are educated, wealthy, uneducated or poor, we all stand before God made in His image, and with the brokenness of sin. The more time my family has lived in East LA, the more we have realized how beautiful this community is. Our children are going through the public schools here, our friends are here, and we are experiencing Jesus here, in what we now call home.

Among the immigrants and "homies" of East LA, as well as those who have relocated from middle-class lives to be a part of this community, I have witnessed great transformation in the hearts of people I serve. People who were enemies of God—stuck in anger, depression, isolation, fear, and addictions—have been set free. I have seen Matthew chapter four lived out many times in these years. I have witnessed numerous physical healings and demonic deliverances, as well as the awesome power of the kingdom of God. I regularly ask Jesus for more!

Yet I have learned that Jesus desires to develop disciples. His power to heal us is part of our transformation process, but committed discipleship is at the center of this process. Jesus intends to change the world by raising up people who are dedicated to obeying His commands so that their hearts, minds, and lifestyles look like those of their servant-leader and model.

Hearts on the verge of transformation are hungry for the teachings of Jesus, desperate for His life-saving grace, and willing to take the Bible seriously and put the commands and promises of Scripture into action. True transformation happens when people believe in the teachings of Jesus so deeply that they actively live them out. In the end, any revival is nothing without the long and fruitful commitment of discipleship.

There's a scene in the movie *Transformers* where Bumblebee, the old, beat-up Camaro, takes offense when his passengers mock his appearance. He throws them out of the car, leaves, and returns as a brand-new, beautiful yellow Camaro. I saw the movie on opening day, and the theater was packed. In that moment, when Bumblebee drives up for the first time and reveals his transformation, all of us in the theater collectively opened our mouths with one united, "Whoa!" followed by shared laughter. We were all caught with our mouths open, blown away by the utter transformation.

How many Christians today cause this kind of jaw-dropping admiration from friends and family after they begin following Jesus? I'm sad to see so few. Every human being is a broken vessel. Unfortunately, all too often the Christian Church tries to fix the problem with new tires and a paint job, instead of walking people through the Sermon on the Mount and discipleship. Jesus wants to transform our hearts, minds, and souls from the inside out! He wants to wow us with the level of transformation He can bring to our lives and the lives of those around us.

HOW TO USE THIS BOOK

THIS BOOK IS AIMING for the foundations and the heart of living with Jesus. The Bible is its main source—I used the New International Version unless otherwise cited—because the Bible has something to say to *everyone*. Likewise, I did my best to write it so that *everyone* walking toward Jesus, from curious skeptics to seasoned church elders, would find something of value in it.

At the same time, the people I pictured most often as I wrote this book were the committed new believers who participate in my church's Discipleship School. These students come from all over, but mostly from around our inner-city neighborhood. They are diverse in formal education, and as growing Christians, they are eager to learn all they can, every way they can.

We are a unique culture today in how we gather and process information. We simply do not read as our grandparents did. But that doesn't mean we are any less serious about following Jesus. Many of the first disciples did not read very much—they learned through more experiential forms instead—but the important point is that they obeyed what they learned. This book is for those who are ready to do something with what they learn, not just be more prepared for the next spiritual debate. This book is for those who want to roll up their sleeves and get to work on the serious business of transformation.

Each chapter ends with discussion questions to help stir up conversation around different topics. Don't be too locked onto these questions, and feel free to add your own! They're given here to help, not to control. Here are some ways you might use them in reading together:

In Reading Groups

AT MY CHURCH'S Discipleship School, a diverse group of Christians gathers weekly to talk about a book. Each member commits to reading the assigned chapter in time for the next group. Our members have full lives and many don't read that often, so this accountability really helps. The discussions are often fruitful and interesting, and it brings our community close together.

To start a discussion group at your church or community center, begin by getting 2 or 3 committed people to start planning with you. Then, invite others and figure out when the most people are available. The group will be most rewarding if all members give a serious commitment to completing the reading each week.

If you have trouble with members showing up without having finished the reading, you can try a few different things:

- Give simple assignments, such as 'Mark your favorite passage to share."

- Have a rotating discussion leader who should bring questions to ask the group, in addition to presenting the questions at the end of each chapter.

- Get a written commitment from each member that they'll read next time.

- Read key passages out loud together, rather than relying on individual reading.

After checking that everyone has a chance to read, make sure you create a safe space for honest conversation around the topics in the book. Build trust by setting rules around not gossiping outside of the group, and by practicing vulnerability yourself.

In cross-class groups, or groups where some are very experienced Christians and some are just beginning, be sure that everyone is sensitive to the diversity in the group.

Good listening across racial, cultural, and socio-economic difference is not easy—but it is so worth it!

In Pairs

THIS BOOK WAS WRITTEN with discipleship in mind. If you are a more seasoned Christian mentoring or counseling a new believer, this book can be used to guide some fruitful conversation around what it means to be a Christian. I invite both mentors and mentees to be open and vulnerable to each other. Following Jesus for more years does not mean someone has it all figured out, and we have a lot to teach each other!

Many of the same suggestions apply to pairs as to groups: make sure you are both committed to the reading, and create a safe space for discussion. In a discipleship pair, you may be able to dig deeper. Make sure you take time to follow up on your partner's progress if they bring up a big issue.

While I recommend that groups, pairs, and individuals always close and open with prayer, pairs can be especially flexible with when and how much they pray because they can tune into and respond to each other's needs. Take advantage of this: let your reading meeting turn into a prayer session if it seems like that is what you both need.

As Individuals

YOU MIGHT BE READING this book by yourself, and that's okay. But if you are very busy or not used to reading regularly, you might miss the regularity of a partner or group.

Try putting yourself on a schedule or asking someone else to check in on your reading progress from time to time.

You can tell others about what you're reading and you can even bring up the discussion questions in regular conversation. You can ask a pastor, mentor, or friend for advice on how to apply what you've read. All of these things will help you connect with others over the text, even if they can't read with you.

No matter who you're reading with, I invite you to dig deep! Don't leave the words of Jesus on the page—walk by them, wrestling and responding to these challenges in your own life. It's time.

CHAPTER ONE

SIN IS A CANCER

"You have heard that it was said to the people long ago, 'You shall not murder, and anyone who murders will be subject to judgment.' But I tell you that anyone who is angry with a brother or sister will be subject to judgment. Again, anyone who says to a brother or sister, 'Raca,' is answerable to the court. And anyone who says, 'You fool!' will be in danger of the fire of hell."

"You have heard that it was said, 'You shall not commit adultery.' But I tell you that anyone who looks at a woman lustfully has already committed adultery with her in his heart. If your right eye causes you to stumble, gouge it out and throw it away. It is better for you to lose one part of your body than for your whole body to be thrown into hell. And if your right hand causes you to stumble, cut it off and throw it away. It is better for you to lose one part of your body than for your whole body to go into hell."

- Matthew 5:21-22, 27-30

WHEN MY WIFE AND I first moved into East LA, we lived in a small, overcrowded apartment complex. This was very new for me as I had always lived in houses. I was used to a lot of privacy and separation from my neighbors.

Yet here, it was as if we were all living together. I was pushed into a greater depth of relationship. I got to see more deeply what makes us human.

I have fond memories of hanging out on the balcony late at night, laughing with other men in the complex about the frustrations of maintaining our hair styles, playing football in the alleys between the buildings, and barbecuing while listening to music. As soon as our neighbors established that we were trustworthy, we felt as if they had our backs. I experienced a sense of loyalty from new Mexican-American friends that I had not known in previous contexts.

On the other hand, I saw a lot of anger. The walls were thin, so people's business was exposed. The alleys surrounding our complex were dark at night and used by a tiny percentage of people for dangerous activities. On Saturday and Sunday mornings, in order to reach my car, I had to wade through used lighters and walk by a prostitute asleep on a ragged couch. On so many levels, the move to an inner-city apartment was a shock to my system. It wasn't that evil in this complex was any worse than in the middle-class neighborhood I grew up in; it was just more visible. People didn't live in big homes that could hide all their family drama and frustration. Living for many years in this complex helped me understand more about the human condition that exists in all neighborhoods and the ever-present reality of sin.

The reality of my new apartment complex was not a shock to Jesus. Jesus entered and understands the broken human condition better than any of us. He sees our sin and its destructive consequences. In the beginning of the

Great Sermon, He is clear that victims of sin will receive mighty blessings as they follow Him (Matthew 5:2-12). He begins by rallying all those who are broken in spirit, depressed, weak, and sad, those who hunger and thirst for victory in their lives, who long to see mercy win over revenge, who strive for purity and peace, and who are willing to take the blows for following Jesus. He rallies all those who would follow Him and promises that through our trust and obedience to Him, we will change the world. Yet He is not merely an inspirational speaker. Immediately after this rallying cry, He gets practical—*really* practical.

The first practical truth He gives us is that our standards for what we consider healthy and holy are way too low. He reveals this truth by addressing the reality of anger and lust as equivalent sins to murder and adultery (Matthew 5:21-22, 27-30). How does God judge between someone who murders and someone who has an angry thought? He doesn't; they are both guilty. How does God judge between a man who cheats on his wife and a man who looks at another woman and thinks something sexual about her? He doesn't; they are both guilty.

I imagine some of you are a little frustrated right about now. This probably sets off alarms in your mind: How can it be that God judges the one who gets angry in the same way He judges the one who murders? We should ask why this is true, and how this is fair.

WHAT GOD SAYS

JESUS HELPS US understand this tension by giving us a revelation about sin. He says if our eye or our hand is causing us to sin, we should cut it off so that the rest of our body doesn't enter hell (Matthew 5:29-30). Some people, at times, have taken these words literally and cut off all kinds of body parts.[1] Yikes! Thankfully, we know that Jesus is not telling us to literally mutilate our flesh, both from the complete teaching on sin we get from the Sermon on the Mount and from other teachings. (For example, in Mark 7:1-23, He shows that sin is something that comes from the mind and heart, not something that physical action can cure.) While Jesus is not being literal about mutilating flesh, He is being sober about the organic, destructive power of sin.[2]

Back in Jesus' time—first century AD—there was a limit to medical and technological solutions to illness, so doctors would often amputate or "cut off" the infected area before the disease could spread and kill the entire body.[3] To this day, gangrene and deeply infected wounds often require the same treatment. The most common affliction that requires this type of intense, sacrifice-part-for-the-whole kind of treatment is cancer. Cancer is a disease that spreads throughout the body. Every treatment that exists today, in some form or fashion, is attempting to remove the cancerous cells before they spread. Skin cancer and breast cancer are two forms of this deadly disease that often require physical amputation. But even in chemotherapy, the prescribed drugs are killing good parts of the body in order to keep the cancer from spreading. Jesus is telling us that sin is basically *spiritual cancer*. If it is not cut out of our lives, it will grow until it can kill us spiritually.

Sin goes way beyond bad heart attitudes and choices that lead to destruction. Bad behaviors are the symptoms of the root problem: sin, a broken condition of our souls that negatively affects our ability to believe what is true, have joy, and live in line with the heart of God. Any destructive action that we do is not an isolated event, but rather the product of a cancerous condition of our souls that the Bible explains is a part of our very nature at birth.[4]

Now does Jesus' teaching make sense? Murder and anger come from the same root. To kill someone with a gun and to be angry at someone in your mind are both products of the condition of sin that is alive in your soul. They both are the result of your spiritual cancer flaring up. Clearly, there are greater social consequences for actually murdering someone than there are for being angry, as there should be. Someone who murders another person has let their sin cancer grow and dominate their lives to the point of taking another life, but both the murderer and the constantly angry person are living in their sin cancer. Both people are breathing life into evil. Thus, both are guilty before a God who has never been, and will never be, infected with even a speck of sin cancer.

LIFE IN THE CITY

ONE OF THE FIRST GUYS I got to know in our new apartment was Joey. Joey and I were so different. I grew up in the suburbs with both of my parents, both of whom had master's degrees. I spent my teen years playing sports, and at least one of my parents was at every one of my sports games. Joey grew up in the projects with no dad and a not-so-present mother. Joey started to play sports when he was in elementary school, but by middle school he'd started running with a gang. He spent his teenage years learning how to fight and shoot guns. He spent his twenties in jail. I spent my twenties as a campus pastor.

Joey lived a few doors down from me, and one day his wife Andrea was walking past our apartment to go to the laundry machines. Being a hot summer day, our door was open, and my wife and I started talking with her. Joey looked over and could only see me chatting with Andrea. For the next month, I kept wondering why Joey was always mad-dogging me and not responding when I greeted him in passing. Thankfully, his wife and mine became close, and we were invited to their son's birthday party. At one point during the party, Joey, with a little alcohol influence, confessed he had wanted to hurt me for what he perceived as me talking to his wife on that hot summer day. He had actually picked up his knife and started to walk toward my apartment, when suddenly he felt something in his gut that caused him to stop and go back home. As he finished his confession, I mumbled out a traumatized, "Thank you for not killing me." He hugged me about seven times, telling me that I was "legit" and that we were "homies" (slang for friend or brother). From that point forward, we were great friends.

As I got to know Joey, he confided in me that he had a horrible habit. Whenever he was stressed or tired from work or fighting with his wife, he would get his gun and start driving around town, looking for a rival gang member to mess with. He knew it was not a healthy way to deal with his problems. He knew it was destroying his life, and that looking for a fight could get him killed, and yet he couldn't stop. It was an addiction. He loved the rush of a fight. That, along with alcohol, was how he dealt with stress and anger.

At first I didn't know how to respond to Joey in those moments when he vented about this addiction. I didn't know how to be a good friend to him. All I could do was listen and agree that it was time to stop the habit immediately.

About six months into knowing Joey, I got a little more insight into his struggle through a long talk I had with my wife. At the time, our family situation was really difficult. We were raising a two-year-old boy and a newborn baby in a tough apartment complex. My efforts at planting a church were failing, which put me in a depressed state. The long talk I had with Maggie was centered on me "checking out" at home. I would come home from work, usually depressed or unhappy, and definitely not excited to enter into the chaos of dirty diapers, sick babies, and the destruction our two-year-old boy had wrought on our apartment. So I played video games—violent video games. I was stressed, and I was angry, so I killed virtual people until I was tired enough to go to sleep. Sound familiar?

Yes, Joey's actions had greater practical consequences than mine, but our actions came from the same root. Both of us were infected with the same cancer-like condition. Both of us were infected with the same sin. Both of us stood before God, judged and guilty.

GOING FORWARD

WE MUST DEAL WITH, root out, cut off sin. But in order to do that, there are several steps involved.

Own up to sin

THE FIRST STEP in our journey toward a more transformed life is to understand, identify, and own up to our sin. Understanding sin for what it really is—that's the secret to a new life. Once we can see the power of sin, we can then start to deal with its corruption and ability to spread into every part of our lives. But the more we minimize sin's reality, downplay its power, or limit it to "bad actions," the less we'll be able to grow with Jesus. If we're not willing to confront the sin in our own lives and cut it off at its root, then it will eventually consume us.

Sin has always been the most complicated and difficult struggle in human history. We can create a computer that fits in the palm of our hands today, and tomorrow replace it with a gun used to kill innocent people in a movie theater. We can write some of the most soul-stirring poetry, screenplays, and music today, and then tomorrow shred our brother's soul apart in five minutes with some of the most creatively vile words ever invented. We can sacrifice our very lives to save a stranger from a burning building in the morning, and then in the evening not give an ounce of energy to deal with the fire of anger raging in our own home.

We often brag about how far we have evolved as a human society. We display our new technology, our new ideas, and our new fashion. Yet from the first day we have existed until now, we struggle to be able to relate rightly to each other and to God. We have worked so hard to transform the surface, while sin continues to destroy us on the inside.

Sin is a living, breathing condition that we all struggle with. It is the main enemy that prevents us from transforming into people after God's own heart. We must first see sin for what it is—a spiritual cancer. Once we acknowledge and understand our enemy, then we can start working on how to defeat it.

We are easily convinced that our sin is not that big of a deal. Can you imagine how frustrated a doctor would be if you kept disagreeing with her diagnosis of cancer, convinced instead that it was just a common cold? To own up to our sin condition is to submit to Jesus' diagnosis of our problem, instead of dismissing Him as too extreme.

There is freedom in honesty. There is transformation to be found when we own up to our condition. The condition of sin works so hard to convince us that we are fine. Sin wants to stay alive; it wants to continue to dominate your life. So do what any healthy person would do when they realize someone has ill intentions—fight with everything you've got!

Understand the aspect of deceit

SIN IS CHARACTERIZED by deceit. It lies to your soul, heart, and mind; it distorts what is right and truthful. Initially, sin deceives us with a great first impression. Sin rarely approaches as a scary monster, but rather as a smooth, attractive, easy option. We often say yes to that first invitation sin offers. We say yes because we think we have found what our hearts truly desire, and if it's our heart's true desire, it cannot be harmful, right? Wrong. Sin often moves just like a charming, attractive person asking us to dance. We think there is no harm in one little dance, yet we don't realize that we are slowly being danced over to the back door. The only ending is being taken out the back door, and tortured to death in a dark alley.

Scripture is very clear on the dangers of giving in to temptation.[5] The only ending is where sin pulls you deeper and deeper in, so that the final result is eternal spiritual death. Take a deep breath and try to take this in. Spiritual torture, death, and isolation—this is the end awaiting you if you keep letting sin have its way in your life.

Don't fall for cheap grace

ONE WAY THAT SIN has deceived us is by convincing us to play the "grace of God" card in inappropriate ways. It is a golden truth that God's mercy and forgiveness are endless and can cover anything, but God's mercy is not meant to be a crutch, allowing us to ignore the severity of our sinful condition under the pretense that all will be forgiven later.

God calls us to repent of our sins—which includes acknowledging them in the first place—in order to receive forgiveness and the power to heal. Acts 20:21 says, "I have declared to both Jews and Greeks that they must turn to God in repentance and have faith in our Lord Jesus." Sin lies to us by telling us that we can do what we want now and simply be forgiven later, but God calls us to a transformed life. He calls us to live out the commandments (Exodus 20:1-17, John 15:10) and bear spiritual fruit (Galatians 5:22-23, John 15:4), becoming like Christ in our thoughts and deeds (1 John 4:17, 1 Peter 2:21, John 13:15, Matthew 11:29). The mercy of God is not meant to convince us that we just have a common cold, and thus make us lazy people who are unwilling to take the appropriate medicine. Remember, we don't have a cold, or even broken bones; we are infected with a serious cancer.

Cheap grace is saying a prayer, going to church every Sunday, and feeling justified to judge those on reality TV. Cheap grace is believing that your sin is not that big of a deal, because you are "in"—in God's club, on the list for Heaven, covered. Cheap grace avoids truthful examinations of our souls, and concludes that we are actually good people with just a few annoying habits. True grace opens up our eyes to the horrendous nature of our souls and sets us on a lifelong path of humility and freedom.

When we step back and realize what it cost to receive the mercy of God, we should be in utter amazement at the severity of our condition. How do we, as broken humans, even begin to understand that the only cure for our condition was for the eternal source of all love, life, power, and creativity to become human and be tortured and killed by His own creation?

Receive Jesus' help

GRACE IS A GIFT we do not deserve. Grace is a constant, intimate relationship with Jesus in the midst of our sin cancer. Jesus sacrificed His life so that we could be free from sin's destruction. He conquered death and sin and made a way for us to follow Him into victory. These words of His—the Great Sermon—give us the tools and the power to overcome the effect of sin in our lives. Like any parent, Jesus won't sit back and let this enemy keep killing His kids. He has sacrificed everything to save us.

No matter what label we want to put on our sin—issues, brokenness, bad habits—we can never change the severity of the problem, and our inability to overcome it without the love and power of Jesus. Your sin is really that bad. And Jesus' love is really that good.

Fight against sin by cutting off what needs to be cut off

AFTER TALKING WITH MY WIFE about my addiction to the violent video games, I finally realized how anger was damaging my soul. I saw how sin cancer was growing through each violent game I played. I knew that I had to obey Jesus and cut off the rotten "limb." So I gave away my gaming system. It has been ten years since then, and I have never missed it. The "cutting off" of the system was simply the first of many steps I needed to take to become a husband and father who does not allow my sin cancer to affect my family. I am a different husband and father today than I was then, yet I am still growing, still in a battle to keep sin from messing up my life. Joey is still alive, currently working his first full-time job, faithful to Andrea and their kids, and moving away from destructive living. Jesus is a great doctor!

Fight against sin by being accountable

DURING ANOTHER DIFFICULT SEASON, I remember calling a friend every single night to check in until that particular temptation was no longer trying to ruin my life. Of course, calling someone every night so they could check my behavior was rather humiliating. There were times before dialing the number where I would feel frustrated or annoyed, like I was in prison or on probation, but that is exactly the problem! We hate facing reality when that reality reveals something negative within us; we don't want to believe that we are sick, or a danger to ourselves and the people around us. Sin inflames our pride, and we begin to convince ourselves that we don't need healing or help.

Some people argue that setting up practical consequences for sin or bringing in peers for accountability relationships leads to legalism and competition. Of course it can—we can twist anything into an evil. We also have a funny way of talking and exegeting our way out of obeying Jesus. But Jesus says to live in such a way that you are a walking, mutilated, free person, eternally bound for a new life. Scripture commands us to confess our sin to others, and help each other every day in this journey.[6] If setting up practical consequences and having an accountability partner help us live out this calling, then by all means, let's do it. The point of being a disciple of Jesus is that people can see our theology being worked out in the practical aspects of our lives.

Fighting sin is exhausting. I have learned that Jesus' call to be radical in fighting sin can often be more difficult for those of us who are older in age and further along in our journey with God. Sin never completely goes away. It is built into our nature. It is like weeds in our garden, or cockroaches in our kitchen. We're energized for the fight initially, but when we realize it is going to be a lifelong fight, we try to find ways to get around it.

Instead, we must get on our knees and ask Jesus for a new kind of humility—a humility that will overcome the sin of pride that stops us from seeking help, a humility that will radically change how we live our lives. We need to stay vigilant and practical. Sin is more deceitful than presidential candidates in televised debates. Sin will tell you whatever you need to hear to let it live. We can't be deceived any longer. We must fight against sin's pull toward the alley. We must fight against the cancer that seeks our destruction.

QUESTIONS TO CONSIDER

1. In this chapter, we saw that sin like uncontrolled anger can show up in many different ways. Joey's anger showed up in the big, obvious sin of taking out a gun and looking for people to mess with. My anger showed up in a less obvious way: through violent video games. Share a way that sin shows up in your actions, whether it's an obvious 'sin' or not.

2. What's hard about owning up to your sin cancer? Do you find yourself assuming that certain types of people or certain neighborhoods have greater sin than your own? Do you believe that owning up to your sin cancer is crucial to your growth?

3. Cheap grace is grace that doesn't cost you anything, and doesn't require you to address your sin cancer. How has cheap grace shown up in your church, your family, your life?

[1] Matt Kuelfer, "The Practice of Self-Castration in Early Christianity," *Trans Christians*, accessed November 29, 2016, *www.transchristians.org/archive/the-practice-of-self-castration-in-early-christianity*.

[2] Jesus often uses hyperbole and intense language to prove or emphasize His point. See Matthew 23:23-24, Matthew 7:3-5, and Mark 10:24-25 as examples.

[3] Earl E. Vanderwerker, Jr., "A Brief Review of the History of Amputations and Prostheses," *The Inter-Clinic Information Bulletin* 15, no. 5 (1976): 15-16.

[4] Isaiah 53:6, Psalm 51:5, Psalm 58:3, Romans 8:3, Colossians 3:5-10. For a thorough look at the biblical teaching on sin, consider J. C. Ryle, *Holiness* (Durham, UK: Evangelical Press, 1995).

[5] Genesis 4:7, Mark 9:42-48, John 5:14, 1 Peter 5:8.

[6] James 5:16, Hebrews 3:12-14, 1 John 1:5-10, Matthew 6:9-13.

CHAPTER TWO

YOUR HEAVENLY FATHER LOVES YOU

"Look at the birds of the air; they do not sow or reap or store away in barns, and yet your heavenly Father feeds them. Are you not much more valuable than they?"

- Matthew 6:26

"If you, then, though you are evil, know how to give good gifts to your children, how much more will your Father in heaven give good gifts to those who ask him!"

- Matthew 7:11

HAVE YOU EVER THOUGHT about what makes you most happy? What gives you the deepest and most sustaining joy? If you think hard, you'll probably find that the answer is love.

My dad started a tradition in our family that I have since carried on with mine. Every so often, I choose someone at the dinner table to be honored. Each family member then takes a turn telling that person why they love them and what is so special about them. My favorite part of this "love session" is watching the kids' reactions when I announce it. The older kids are, the more they react with embarrassment, but it's only a few minutes before you see the deep joy on their faces.

As family members take turns loving on them, I can see their mind, heart, and soul being filled up with love. Usually, when we are done with dinner, the one who has been honored is most excited to help clean up and serve. It makes sense, doesn't it? When your "love tank" is full, it is easier to love others. When it is empty, we focus on taking care of ourselves and getting some more love.

One of the themes of the Great Sermon is the love of God our Father. I've found that it is easy to miss this theme because I am so fixated on how hard the Great Sermon is to obey, and how much I need to work on my discipleship. But you see it laced throughout the text—Jesus keeps coming back to our relationship with our heavenly Father. It seems to me that Jesus is redefining our image of God. He is trying to help us see that God is the greatest Father we could ever imagine—even beyond our imagination. He is the good father you never had, infinitely greater than the earthly father you do have. Jesus is most clear about this in Matthew 7:11: "If you, then, who though you are evil [infected with sin cancer], know how to give good gifts to your children, how much more will your Father who is in heaven give good gifts to those who ask him!"

Jesus is contrasting human fathers and God, and He did not pick an alcoholic, absent father to compare; He chose a healthy father, one who gives good gifts. Yet even the best earthly fathers cannot compare to the perfection of God our Father.

Many of us have wounds from our mothers and fathers, areas of need because of the way our earthly parents did not provide the love we needed. In some ways, these wounds want to define us. But I want to be clear about something: your earthly mother or father can't fix all your wounds. While we need to hold dads and moms to their responsibility as parents, we also need to return to the rock solid truth that ONLY God our heavenly Father can meet all of our needs. Only God our heavenly Father can deal with our sin cancer. Only God our heavenly Father can transform our lives into so much more. Only God our heavenly Father can heal our father and mother wounds.

WHAT GOD SAYS

DID YOU NOTICE the repetition in Matthew 5-7 of God, your Father, giving you good things?[7] It strikes me that this truth is repeated in the context of such an incredibly challenging sermon. In the midst of challenging us to look at how sick we are and how much we need to change, Jesus keeps reminding us that our Father loves us! Even in the midst of our rebellion, even in the midst of our problems, God loves us! It is clear that Jesus is trying to counter our instinct to view God as an angry, disappointed, strict Father. We see this kind of correction most strongly in His teaching on worry, where Jesus is essentially saying, "Hey, what are you thinking? God loves the birds, and you are a hundred times more valuable to Him than the birds! There is nothing in His created order that is more special to Him than you!"

One of the horrific symptoms of our sin-infested souls is that we believe the lie that God does not love us, that

He does not want to give us good things, and that He is not with us. We quickly slip into living as if Jesus were a strict teacher who won't help us with our homework and who will only be happy if we turn in a perfect test. Or we live as if Jesus were some cosmic police officer, protecting the universe and happily busting us for our crimes.

As a broken person, I have learned that one of the most important, life-sustaining habits is to regularly receive my heavenly Father's love for me. I can never have enough! Our heavenly Father's love is the greatest medicine to heal our sin cancer. Remember the dinner table honoring time? When we are filled up with love, we will love more. When we are secure in God's love for us, we will less likely be tempted to find love through sinful and destructive living.

You were created to constantly need the Father's love. God wants a real relationship with you. He is not the kind of father who visits you once a year for Christmas, gives you a gift, and tells you to "man up" and take care of the family. God wants to hang with you every day. He created you to be healthiest when you are secure in His love. The older I get, the more I want to live in God's presence and love! And the older I get, the more I need His love in my life.

God our Father knows how to show us our weaknesses and where we need to change, while at the same time reinforcing His love for us. It is a balance that good earthly fathers are constantly trying to master with their children. If we only criticize and highlight our children's weaknesses, they become paralyzed, fearful, angry, rebellious, or insecure. Yet if we only accept and affirm them and ignore their mistakes, we raise kids who are spoiled, selfish, and ridiculously unaware of their own sin cancer. As we see in this Great Sermon, God knows how to do both all the time, but in such a way that we actually respond with a desire for transformation.

We can never have enough love from our Father in heaven. We need to help each other regularly drink from this well by reminding each other of the love God has for us, as seen in Scripture, and by loving each other directly. As we look at the Great Sermon, we notice that Jesus continually leads us to love and serve others, even our enemies. In doing so, we model the love of God, which fills up the "love tank" of the other person, who can then go out and love someone else. Christian communities that are centered on honoring, affirming, and practically loving each other are communities that will transform individual lives and be shining lights in the world.

Jesus begins His summary of the Great Sermon by saying, "So in everything, do to others what you would have them do to you, for this sums up the Law and the Prophets" (Matthew 7:12). He is basically saying that if you have a hard time remembering all the ways He wants you to change, sum it all up with this "Golden Rule." One of the things we most desire as human beings is for others to tell us why we are valuable. Not much else fills up the love tank more deeply than thoughtful words of honor.

LIFE IN THE CITY

PEOPLE IN THE CITY do not need any more drive-by ministries. They are not looking for more flashy words, free handouts, and weekend programs. They are looking for something real. It is so important that those called to minister in the city actually live in the city. Jesus did not stay in the comforts of heaven and drive through our chaotic world every once in a while. I am often surprised by the observations people in my neighborhood make about my life. I once had a young man say, "I have never seen a marriage like yours. Your marriage gives me hope that I too can have a good marriage someday." My marriage is not perfect, but it certainly has been molded by Jesus. In fact, it almost never happened. I was on a path to add to the divorce statistics.

If I could change one thing about my teenage years, it would be deciding not to date. I blindly followed the norms of my peers and did not have healthy relationships. I made a lot of mistakes and hurt some people. At twenty years old, I finally owned up to this. I owned up to a lot of things at twenty, because that was when I decided to let God lead my life. I stopped dating altogether to heal, deal, and learn about life with Jesus. I knew that I had a long way to go before I was ready to be a good husband.

Fast forward to my wedding day. I was now twenty-six. Maggie came into my life three years after not dating anyone. I almost messed up the relationship initially, but then fully committed to obeying all the kingdom principles Jesus pressed upon me. I began to experience a relationship that I never knew could exist. Eventually, it was a no-brainer to ask Maggie to marry me.

Five minutes before it was time to walk to the altar and say my vows, I was in the back room with my groomsmen and pastor. I was exploding with anxiety and excitement, as there were over four hundred people to witness our vows! My pastor said, "It's almost time, so let's gather around Chris and pray for him." As my friends put their hands on my shoulders, my pastor suggested I pray first.

I took a deep breath, closed my eyes, and saw a picture in my mind: a huge hand came out of the sky and placed Maggie in front of me. Then I heard, "I love you, Chris. This marriage is one of my greatest gifts to you." That picture rocked my world. In an instant, I flashed back to the broken man I was in high school, and saw how the only thing my actions and dating history would have earned me was a dysfunctional marriage that would end in divorce. Yet here I was, about to enter into a lifelong covenant with a woman who was a gift to me from my heavenly Father.

There is nothing more intense than getting in touch with your sin and God's love at the same time! The only words I got out of my mouth were, "Thank you so much, God," and then I started weeping. My friends and pastor let me be in the moment for a few seconds, and then, in my ear, my dad started praying for me. What a moment! He wasn't there when we started; he was sitting in the first row, waiting for things to begin. But he felt a nudge in his soul to find me and pray for me before the ceremony. He walked in on me crying, and my best man let my dad replace his hand on my shoulder. To experience the love of my heavenly Father and my dad at the same time was wonderful. I felt such an overflow of love. "If you, then, though you are evil, know how to give good gifts to your children, how much more will your Father in heaven give good gifts to those who ask him!"

GOING FORWARD

WE ALL WANT TO LIVE in this love. So practically, how do we get closer to the love that God is outpouring on us?

Recognize that God is our life source

FIRST, WE NEED to realize that regularly receiving God's love is our life source. As we walk through the Great Sermon, we will see that Jesus is asking us to make a lot of significant changes in our lives. In fact, the depth of the transformation He calls us to is going to overwhelm us. Our first reaction may be, "I just can't do this!" It is okay to say that. In fact, we cannot accomplish the changes Jesus asks of us on our own. We are too selfish, too addicted, too moody, too weak, and too forgetful. We can change on our own in some ways, but when we realize we can't fully live up to the standard Jesus lays out, we may try to justify lowering the standard so that we don't feel as guilty. But in the end, Jesus keeps bringing us back to His Great Sermon standard.

I am convinced that He purposefully calls us to a life that we can't achieve on our own, so that must rely on Him. His hint at this "impossibility" is found at the beginning of the Great Sermon. In Matthew 5:20 He says, "For I tell you that unless your righteousness surpasses that of the Pharisees and the teachers of the law, you will certainly not enter the kingdom of heaven." The people He references here—Pharisees—were known for their righteous, law-abiding lives. But what they did, they did by their own power. Jesus calls us to an even higher standard, one that we can only achieve with His help. In the Great

Sermon, Jesus gives us a lot of practical commands, but He ends with the command to ask our heavenly Father for all good things (Matthew 7:7-11). The only way to live a transformed life is to be in a real relationship with God, where we ask Him for everything we need. In the end, Jesus is asking us to see his reality: we are children and need our Father's guidance, wisdom, strength, and power. How very different from what the streets will tell us—that our joy and freedom in life are found when we don't need anyone to help us!

Imagine what would happen if an eight-year-old boy told his parents that he wanted a one-way ticket to a different state to live independently from them. Without the guidance of his parents, his life would quickly become a train wreck. Without God our Father as the primary influence in our lives, we quickly become train wrecks. The secret to obeying the Great Sermon, and therefore living a transformed life of joy, is to own up to the reality of being a child and to always remain in our Father's house. He is the best Father, never manipulative, never forceful; He is a generous Father, always excited to shower us with love; and He is a strong Father, able to destroy any hindrance to a healthy life. Drinking in the Father's love is utterly necessary, and striving to stay in relationship with God is the most important pursuit of our lives. Our relationship with God is our power-base. Everything else flows from this point of strength.

Spend time with God as a means of avoiding the spiral of sin

REMEMBER HOW NASTY our sin cancer is. It is actively trying to deceive us all the time by saying, "You are not that bad." But Jesus is trying to tell us, "Actually you are that bad! You are all messed up!" We don't realize how powerful sin is. All it takes is a little spark, and our day spirals out of control. We need to understand that the horrible fight you just had, or the funk that is crippling your soul, is not an isolated event. When we fail to treat our sin cancer, we get into negative cycles.

For example, you're lying in bed at night, angry at your spouse because of a fight you just had. You realize that the fight was not an isolated event, but the result of a cycle of poor choices. The night before, you were really tired around 10 pm. But you got caught up watching late-night TV and sat with your eyes glossed over and drool coming out of your mouth for two hours. You fell asleep on the couch, woke up at 2 am, and stumbled to your bed. Your alarm went off at 6 am. You were a zombie, so you hit the snooze button three times. The fourth time it went off, you jumped out of bed, swearing, because you were going to be late. You pulled your clothes on, grabbed a crappy breakfast, snapped at your kid who was making you even later by wanting to show you a crayon drawing of a dinosaur. You ran to the car or bus stop and got angry because traffic was slow or the bus was late. You turned on talk radio and listened to grown men yell at each other. You got to work and had twenty emails to answer, or one hundred beams to install, or 200 students to teach.

So when you came home at 7 pm and your spouse said, "I didn't like how you yelled at the baby this morning," instead of owning up to your stuff and apologizing, you had absolutely no love in your tank and entered into a ten-round fight. You finally walked away and sat in front of the TV again, hoping to escape your reality for a few hours. At midnight, the cycle started all over again.

It is time to sober up. Our sin cancer is slowly destroying our lives. Late-night TV is not going to give you what you need. CNN, ESPN, and the morning news are not going to set you up for a day of love, forgiveness, humility, joy, and seeking first the kingdom of God!

Try to imagine how incredibly different your day would be if just two things changed: One. You went to bed earlier and got a good night's sleep. Two. You woke up thirty to sixty minutes before you needed to and spent time with your heavenly Father. In this time with God, you are reminded of how good He is, how powerful He is, how much He loves you and wants to give you good things. You are reminded that life is about loving your family and the people you interact with daily. In this time, you sing to Him, you read His Word, and you pray for your kids. After your time with God, you go and wake up your children with joy and a full tank of love. I don't think I need to spell out the rest of the day for you, but it looks a lot better than the previous example, doesn't it?

We can talk all we want about loving Jesus, but what does your daily life say? If Jesus is first, give Him the first part of your day. Anchor your day on Him. If you really believe His word and promises, then do what He says! As I look back over the last ten years of my life, the decision to commit—no excuses—to spending time with God every morning is the best practical change I have made in my life by far. It prepares me to obey the commands of the Great Sermon.

Be persistent

IT WON'T ALWAYS feel good. There are mornings when my heart is alive, I feel God, I hear Him speak directly to me through His Word, and I come away feeling on fire. But that is not the norm. Many days it is a struggle to keep my heart within God's heart. I am nodding off to sleep, zoning out, or unable to get my mind off the pressures of the day. On the toughest of days, when I can't seem to get connected, I say this prayer, "Father, I know you are with me. I put myself on your operating table. Do whatever it takes to heal me and connect my heart and mind to you."

I have learned that daily time with Jesus is like physical exercise. You won't see instant results, and you won't see results every day. But over time, if you keep "working out," you will see a difference. Over time, I have seen myself grow in patience, servanthood, perseverance, and openness about my faith. Our faith—which includes our daily practices—should be based on truth, not on our passing emotions. Life is not a sprint; it is a marathon.

Pick a time and place to pray

DON'T WAIT TO DECIDE on a place to pray until the morning, when you're tired and would rather stay in bed. Find a private place where you feel comfortable being vulnerable. The point is to come to God without a mask on, to be open about your anger, doubts, insecurities, and anxieties. Choose a place where you can lay all of this on the table without looking over your shoulder to see who else is watching. Come to God like a small child does with their parents, holding nothing back.

Plan your bed time based upon your time with God

DECIDE HOW MUCH TIME you want to spend with God, and thus what time you need to wake up. Then figure out how much sleep you need and set a strict bedtime. As adults, we hate living with rules and limitations. We love to believe that we deserve complete "freedom." Then we wonder why we keep walking in circles without any real change. To this day, I have nights where I wrestle with my flesh over going to bed early instead of vegging out in front of the TV. But every morning when I wake up early to spend quality time with my great Father, I realize once again that He is so much better.

Be flexible

WHILE WE CAN SET a bedtime, life is not always lived in a controlled rhythm. Crises happen, and we need to be flexible. We should never reject the act of loving people because we have to get to bed at a certain time. In Matthew 5:23-25, Jesus shows us that loving people is integrated into loving Him. Yet it is fighting for those consistent, daily times with Jesus that gives us what we need to sacrifice in order to love others.

Remember that God will provide

GOD IS NOT a harsh manager. I find that God often surprises me with rest I didn't think I would get. A meeting gets cancelled and I get a power nap, or I get to catch up on sleep during my days off. On those days, I still try to spend the first hour of my day with God, but I get to start that hour later. We are not making this commitment to prove something to God and others. We are not doing it because we are afraid of being punished. We are doing it because we are sick, and we are tired of going around in circles, struggling with the same issues over and over again because we are too afraid of going "all in" with Jesus.

Persevere

AT FIRST, IT WILL be difficult to persevere. We often jump right into something because we are excited to try something new, but then the suffering will start—it won't feel so good, it will get boring, you will feel tired, your heart will start to grumble, etc. This is the sin cancer in us. In order to persevere, it is helpful to seek help and accountability. You will need to identify all the excuses and tricks that your sick heart is coming up with.

When I first started my daily time with Jesus, we were living in our small apartment in East LA. There was literally no place to pray in private in our apartment. The building was so old that the walls were paper thin, and people don't enjoy being woken up by singing at six in the morning. I was excited to jump in, but quickly started feeling the suffering and the inconvenience. I wanted to stop trying, and I thought my best excuse was that there was nowhere to pray. I remember thinking, "Well, God, if you get us a bigger place, I can start praying early in the morning."

Eventually Jesus got through to my sick, excuse-making heart. I realized there was a place I could pray in private: my car. So for a long time, in the dark, early mornings, I would walk down three flights of stairs to the carport. The front passenger seat became my little spiritual home. I always wondered what my neighbors thought when they saw me in the car during those early mornings: "That white boy is struggling in his marriage; he can't even sleep on the couch!"

Be prepared to change the routine

YOU MIGHT NEED to change your routine in order to keep your time with God feeling fresh. Sometimes I walked around a big park in my neighborhood, talking out loud to God. At first I was a little self-conscious, but my time with God was more important than what people thought about me.

Some suggestions regarding prayer

PEOPLE OFTEN ASK ME how to pray. Prayer, like anything, takes time to learn. If you have never really prayed longer than a pre-meal kind of prayer, you need to realize that it is going to take some time to feel comfortable. We are all wired differently. I have an intense, extroverted, emotionally charged personality, so it doesn't help me to spend all my time in silence. I do need time to be silent, to listen to God, but I also need to get loud and messy and raw. Singing is really helpful for me, so I make sure singing is always a part of the time I spend with God.

No matter how we are wired, we always need the Bible because we always need to be reminded of what is true. The way to counter sin, which is deceitful at its root, is to read truth daily. Some people like to spend their time in a sort of free-flow, while others like strict structure. I like a mix of both. Take some time to think about what you need, and then spend time trying different ways to come before God. Just as a way to get started, I'll share the general flow of my personal morning time with God.

I start the time by honoring and praising God, verbally telling Him who He is. He doesn't need to hear it, but I need to say it. Often, as I list the characteristics of God, one will hit me hard. Maybe on that particular day I need to sit on that specific character trait of God. So when I say, "You are in control of all things!" I might pause, realize that my heart does not believe that right now, and begin to work through my unbelief by pulling God's sovereignty deeper into my being. Every day with God is different, because we enter the time from very different places, and God will use the time in unique ways.

I confess any sin that I am aware of. I get it all out. This leads me to cry out to God again for mercy, acknowledging that I am nothing without Him.

After confession, I spend time trying to take in His love. Sometimes this takes one minute; sometimes it takes twenty. Generally, this is the time I start singing. Singing songs to God helps me figure out the condition of my heart. Sometimes I need to stop singing in order to deal with pain or anxiety, but often this is the time I feel joyful in God. My goal is to remain with my heavenly Father until I am satisfied in Him, until I know that His love is with me for the day. This might not always be a feeling, but it will always be a truth that can be accepted with conviction.

I spend time praying for people who are on my heart: my family and church, friends who I want to see give their lives to Jesus, areas of injustice that are affecting people in my community, etc.

I spend time in Scripture. Depending on the season of life, I will either read through one specific book of Scripture over and over, or work my way through the Bible with the help of a reading plan.[9]

I spend time listening to God, asking for His direction in both big decisions and daily ones.

If I have time left, I journal to collect my thoughts and cement what God was speaking to me, and then I pray over the day's responsibilities.

If I am in a tough season, I will often ask friends if I can pray with them as a way to reboot my intimacy with my Heavenly Father. In the end, it comes down to what is best for your heart and life. There are multiple ways to approach your Father. If you know the love of God is your life-source, then go all in. Commit to daily time with Jesus, even when you don't feel like it.

QUESTIONS TO CONSIDER

1. As you consider the deep, enduring love of God your heavenly Father, how does this compare and contrast with your relationship to your parents?

2. When have you felt most present with God? In other words, what has your "quality time" with God looked like in the past?

3. What changes can you make to spend more time with God? Are you willing to commit to those changes now?

---

[7] Matthew 5:45, 6:4, 6:6, 6:14, 6:18.
[8] Genesis 1:26, Psalm 8:4-8, Luke 12:7, Psalm 139:14, Matthew 10:29-31.
[9] One idea is *The One Year Bible NIV* (Carol Stream, IL: Tyndale, 2015). Many websites also give reading plans. Try *www.biblegateway.com/reading-plans/* to get started!

CHAPTER THREE

THE JOURNEY TOWARD GENUINE HUMILITY

*"Blessed are the poor in spirit, for theirs
is the kingdom of heaven...*

Blessed are the meek, for they will inherit the earth."

- Matthew 5:3, 5

*"Do not judge, or you too will be judged. For in the same
way you judge others, you will be judged, and with
the measure you use, it will be measured to you."*

*"Why do you look at the speck of sawdust in your broth-
er's eye and pay no attention to the plank in your own
eye? How can you say to your brother, 'Let me take
the speck out of your eye,' when all the time there is
a plank in your own eye? You hypocrite! First take
the plank out of your own eye, and then you will see
clearly to remove the speck from your brother's eye."*

- Matthew 7:1-5

THERE ARE QUITE A FEW people in our church who are in
recovery from various addictions. Those who have been
through Alcoholics Anonymous (AA) or Narcotic Anonymous (NA) are some of the most inspirational friends in

my life. When I hang around them, I often feel that I am in the presence of God.

I am always schooled in genuineness and humility. My friends in recovery have a deep acceptance of sin: they're done trying to convince themselves and others that their problems are no big deal. For those accustomed to building their identity on educational degrees, career status, and home remodels, the bluntness and rawness of people in recovery can often be shocking.

One of my most inspirational friends is a woman we will call Victoria. She has been sober from hard drugs for over a decade. Her husband is still an addict, which keeps her life in constant chaos. Victoria comes to church every week, and every week she is an open book. Once, in a joint conference with people from different churches, she stood up in front of strangers and said, "My husband doesn't think I am attractive. He watches porn and won't be with me. I have been depressed and angry for a while, but God just spoke to me yesterday and said that I can be secure in Him. He knows I am beautiful. And He is starting to work on the hearts of my adult children. I know that soon they will be walking with Jesus." (They are both following Jesus as I write this.)

It is hard to convey the tone of her sharing in this moment. But the room was inspired and in awe. Victoria went from one moment of sharing pain to sharing the hope for her kids in Jesus. She shows me Jesus more than any preacher on a stage. One of my mentors says, "All of God's best friends are humble people." As I hang out with humble people like Victoria, I stay close to God.

WHAT GOD SAYS

IT IS TRAGIC AND IRONIC that the Christian church in America, in general, is less and less characterized by grace. Jesus' words in Matthew 7, quoted at the beginning of this chapter, need to be held up again and again to stem the tide of judgment. Humanity, outside of real transformation by the Holy Spirit, has always been and will always be judgmental. Sin's strongest weapon is deceit. It works to convince us that we are okay, and the best way to do so is to find other people whom we judge to be worse.

Jesus addresses judgmental attitudes and pride in Matthew 7. Jesus tells us that we see specks in our neighbor's eye while there is a plank in ours (Matthew 7:3). Why wouldn't He reverse it, saying that we see a plank in our neighbor's eye while there's a speck in our own? Or why wouldn't He just say that we both have planks? It seems Jesus is trying to counter the momentum of judgment by helping us to see the severity of our own sin before even thinking about looking at another's. In fact, He humbles us by suggesting that our own sin may be even greater than our neighbor's. In this moment, Jesus makes one of the many sober, conditional, eternal statements that we see throughout the Sermon on the Mount. He says that when we judge our neighbor—believer or not—we bring judgment on ourselves. He is not only referring to how we ought to act within Christian community, but to a universal way of relating to people.

LIFE IN THE CITY

WE WERE IN THE MIDDLE of a Sunday service and had just finished our singing. I walked up to the front of our two-year-old church, prepared to lead eighty people in a time of learning and hearing through the Word of God. I had been performing this function of leadership for fifteen years, but I had no idea what I was about to witness.

At the time, instead of traditional sermons, we would have people sit in groups of three to five. We read a passage of Scripture together, and I, or another member of our teaching team, facilitated a large group discussion. We asked a few questions, people talked in their groups, and then we walked around the room with a cordless microphone. We alternated between small group discussion and large group sharing.

We had spent over one year walking slowly through the Gospel of Mark. On this particular Sunday, we were studying the moment when Jesus was taken by Roman soldiers just prior to His death; He was jumped, arrested, mocked, tortured, and dishonored (Mark 15:16-20). The conversation around this passage escalated into a very intense and passionate discussion.

Our church is a community-based church in East LA. Of the eighty people in the room, there were about ten immigrant Spanish-speaking adults, a dozen or more teenagers, ten to fifteen adults who had relocated from a middle-class lifestyle to live in the inner-city, and a wide range of Mexican-American adults. Almost every person in the room had grown up on the streets.

Things got tense in the room when one person stood up and asked, "Why didn't Jesus say or do anything? He is getting punked." By the end of our time, we were all trying to grasp the almost impossible leadership of Jesus in this situation. People were struggling to trust the model of Jesus. Some were unsure whether they wanted to believe that he was fully God, some wondered whether they would have had the courage to act in the same way, and others felt a connection with Jesus over similar abuse experiences.

The conversation got to the point where I did not know how to close the time. I stood, looking out at intense faces and feeling my own internal emotional struggle. So I did what I felt I needed to do in that moment: I repented. I wasn't sure how to lead eighty people, but I knew how I needed to lead myself. In my closing prayer, I just said, "I'm sorry." I said sorry to Jesus for living in ways that put me on the side of the soldiers who beat him, for wanting to fight for my rights, for wanting to fight for strength, for mocking those who were weak, for not having the faith to trust that God could rescue me in the midst of social, mental, emotional, and physical persecution. As I finished praying, one of my leaders whispered in my ear, "Ask other people to pray." I did. And for the next twenty minutes, we entered into the presence of Jesus.

Even with eighty people in the room, people stood up, one at a time, and began confessing to Jesus. Some shouted with anger at themselves, some could not finish because tears consumed them, and some dealt with their shame in very quiet voices. People were raw and honest. Parents confessed how they screamed at their children, men confessed a desire to be violent, and teens confessed a lack of desire to forgive. All were begging Jesus for His strength to absorb evil and return love.

I will never forget that Sunday. While not the regular occurrence, it has begun a work within our community of real humility. Humility and honesty are the foundation of any real life transformation.

GOING FORWARD

IT IS SO DIFFICULT to live in humility. It is easy to be kind and nice; it is easy to avoid bragging and overt arrogance. But it is not easy to have a genuine humility of heart.

The myth of holiness

ONE OF THE GREAT myths of the church is that the longer a person walks with Jesus, the more holy they become— holy being understood as "without sin." We see this all the time. When new Christians confess intense sins and are so raw and open about their desperate need for change, we understand, but were someone "older" in the faith to act this same way, there is often judgment for breaking subtle expectations.

People who have been in the faith longer are expected to live cleaner lives. It's okay to talk about certain areas of struggle—anxiety, stress, dryness with God, going through the motions, etc.—but nothing that might seem too weak, needy, or desperate. Those struggles, this false expectation says, should have been conquered already. It can be difficult to remain in a place of desperation, weakness, and humble willingness to bring others into the personal "mess" of sin when faced with the pride of looking good, like you have all your struggles under control. But Jesus says that we are to always find the log in our own eye first. Sharing your sins with God and with your brothers and sisters brings humility, and in humility lies healing and hope.

True growth in Jesus produces true transformation. Accepting the Holy Spirit and obeying the Word of God through the power of the Holy Spirit bring us to a place of transformation where sin no longer dominates our lives. So much so that I can hardly recognize my twenty-year-old self! However, the sin condition, while no longer dominant, still remains. It can flare up in powerful ways at any time. The closer we get to the light, the more we are able to see all the nasty details of our sin cancer. The real transformation I have seen in my selfish, addicted-to-the-flesh, emotionally unstable, broken self is miraculous.

But I am not the one who has been doing the healing. Obeying Jesus' words in the Sermon on the Mount is the secret to change, but obeying His words is simply like taking my medicine. A patient recovering from surgery would never believe that they fixed themselves. I am doing my part by obeying God, opening myself up for His healing touch, and then God can enter my heart and start healing it. However, I have to keep fighting with vigilance for my entire life. I must never stop taking my medicine. The sin condition is such that it hides in deep recesses and will flare up at the first sign of laziness.

The journey with Jesus makes us more aware of how dangerous, potent, and destructive our sin cancer is. Thus, we need to grow in humility, letting go of pride, apathy, or a sense of arrival. Jesus' teaching in Matthew 7—that we are to remove the plank in our own eye before seeing the speck in our brother's eye—reveals that the greatest proof of our humility is how we relate to everyone else.

Frustration with others

THERE ARE MANY WAYS in which our sin cancer prevents us from living in humility. One way is when we become people who are increasingly frustrated with others for their habitual problems. We can understand someone messing up a couple of times, but when that person keeps messing up, over and over and over, it is easy for us to judge and maybe even question their sincerity to change. We seem to forget the times in our lives when we were the repeat offender, and we are blind to the habitual ways we live in sin right now.

Maybe your sin patterns are not obvious to everyone else, or maybe you have seen victory in one area of habitual sin. But sit down with anyone who knows you well, and within ten minutes, they can show you an area in your life where you dishonor the heart of God in regular, habitual ways. Choose into a new kind of humility. Investigate your life and own up to the habitual ways in which you think, feel, or act contrary to the heart of God, and start working on rectifying those problems rather than judging others. We all need to hear the truth about our habitual problems and refusal to change. Yet we need to hear the truth from a humble person who is letting others challenge them as well.

Judging others

A SECOND WAY in which our sin cancer prevents us from living in humility is that we react to our neighbor's sin too quickly. We put people into categories too fast, trusting our own judgment above all else. If we really believe in the biblical view of sin, then we need to realize that we are unable to properly analyze sin in others. It is impossible for us to understand the severity of sin and evil in another person because we are judging them from a place of sickness.

A blind person cannot tell the difference between a masterpiece and one of my stick drawings. What right do we have to blindly assess another person? We know that God hates sin, even a speck of it, so we should spend our energy on living in a place of true humility rather than judging another infected person. Let God be the judge, truly and solely!

Confess our sin

CHURCH LEADERS ESPECIALLY need to hear this word. We need to take drastic risks and courageous steps to usher true kingdom humility into our communities of faith. True communities of humility are not controlled; they are messy. We have to become leaders in the mess and desperately cut off this sin-influenced need for control.

That great Sunday service of confession didn't magically appear out of nowhere. Four months before this service, the twenty-five core leaders of our church went away for a two-day retreat. The goal was to grow in kingdom leadership skills. In the first session, I began our time with a devotion from Revelation 3:14-22. Here is an excerpt: "You say, 'I am rich; I have acquired wealth and do not need a thing.' But you do not realize that you are wretched, pitiful, poor, blind and naked" (Revelation 3:17). I actually wasn't planning on using this Scripture, but earlier that morning, God had burned it into my heart.

I encouraged our young leadership team that we would amount to nothing unless we could be honest and humble with each other. I then proceeded to tell them that I was not a pastor who always lived in the right spirit. I told them about those times in my week when all I wanted to do was escape from reality through watching movies, when I was feeling really cranky and critical, when I argued with my wife, when I snapped at my kids and yelled, or said things I regretted.

I told them that before we could move forward, I needed to be honest with them. I needed help to fight the sin cancer in me. I then encouraged people to stand up and be honest with each other. I explained that being a leader in this church doesn't mean that we can start pretending we have it all together.

We ended up scrapping our agenda for the retreat as my "little devotion" took the entire weekend. It took all weekend for every person to stand before their peers and share honestly. After this vulnerable yet powerful weekend, many leaders told me that any doubts they had about committing to each other and to the mission of our church were erased. We began to lead in humility, offering the larger church family the freedom to own up to their sin cancer and begin an honest, lifelong fight for transformation.

Four months later, this new spirit climaxed in that church service. Messy, yet free. Raw, yet transformative. All of God's best friends are humble people. My brothers and sisters in East LA are real, humble, homies of God.

QUESTIONS TO CONSIDER

1. How can following Jesus make you a more humble person?

2. When have you hurt others by judging them?

3. Is there any confession that you need to make to a supportive Christian mentor or group?

CHAPTER FOUR

OBEDIENCE FIRST

*"Not everyone who says to me, 'Lord, Lord,' will enter the
kingdom of heaven, but only the one who does the will
of my Father who is in heaven. Many will say to me on
that day, 'Lord, Lord, did we not prophesy in your name
and in your name drive out demons and in your name
perform many miracles?' Then I will tell them plainly, 'I
never knew you. Away from me, you evildoers!'"*

*"Therefore everyone who hears these words of mine and puts
them into practice is like a wise man who built his house
on the rock. The rain came down, the streams rose, and
the winds blew and beat against that house; yet it did not
fall, because it had its foundation on the rock. But everyone
who hears these words of mine and does not put them into
practice is like a foolish man who built his house on sand.
The rain came down, the streams rose, and the winds blew
and beat against that house, and it fell with a great crash."*

- Matthew 7:21-27

ONE OF THE MOST repeated themes in the New Testament
is that the love of God, which we receive through the grace
of Jesus, is our great inheritance.[10] Specifically, the very
riches we deeply desire are found in a trusting relationship

with Jesus where we obey all that He commands. Sadly, many people do not see themselves as wealthy in Jesus. Rather, they hope that Jesus will give them whatever they believe to be their dream riches. They often expect Jesus to rubber stamp their own opinions and desires for what they feel will satisfy them, instead of surrendering every part of their lives to Him in complete obedience. While there is no single analogy that can capture every aspect of this reality, consider the following fictional scenario.

Jessica, a simple woman who works as a parking attendant thirty hours a week, is trying to figure out what is next in her life. One afternoon, vegging out to reality TV, her phone rings with an unfamiliar number. She answers and hears, "Hi, Jessica, this is Bill Gates, the richest man in the world. You are my long-lost daughter, and I have worked my entire life to give you everything. I will die tomorrow, and upon my death you will inherit seventy billion dollars. Any time after 9 am tomorrow, please go to the post office with your ID, and they will give you a safe deposit box full of money. It will be there until you pick it up. Enjoy the money! Goodbye."

If we imagine the call is legitimate, there are so many different ways she could use this money. She might buy a big house on a hill, plus a beach house, a cabin in the mountains, and homes for her family members. She might eat all the best food and travel the world, living large. I hope she would remember where she came from, see the global suffering in her travels, and invest tons of this new money to help alleviate suffering. In fact, within ten years of receiving this money, we might see Jessica on the cover of Time magazine. Regardless of what she did with the money, it would completely transform her life.

Grace is the love and forgiveness offered to us by Jesus that we do not deserve, similar to the seventy billion dollars that Bill Gates offered to Jessica. When grace is received and used, it completely transforms our lives in ways that even Gates's money could never do. Grace is never earned, but it must be received and applied.

What if Jessica never went to the post office to pick up the money? What if, over the next several years, she kept telling others that she had the seventy billion dollars, even though she never collected it? Eventually her friends would suspect that she was lying. They would realize that her life had not actually changed since her claims to have these new riches. She hadn't traveled at all; she hadn't given any money to help those in need; she hadn't bought a home; and she was still eating Ramen noodles. Her life had not actually changed because of the gift, as she had never integrated the money into her life. The only change in her life was that she kept telling everyone of her inheritance. Meanwhile, the money, her money, was still waiting for her at the post office! If she continued in this, she would end her life and face God, never having obtained the money.

Many American Christians treat their inheritance from God in this way: they proclaim that they've received this great wealth—salvation, mercy, goodness—but they do little to integrate this gift of grace into their lives. They do not obey all of Jesus' commands. Their lives are not radically changed, and they never share their inheritance with others.

WHAT GOD SAYS

JESUS ENDS THE GREAT Sermon with two very clear teachings on the dangers of not obeying Him. Great teachers give their most important points at the very end, as they know their listeners are more likely to remember the last thing they say. It seems important to focus on the end of the Great Sermon (Matthew 7:21-27) at this point in the book, so that we can take these lessons with us as we study the heart of the sermon. Jesus repeats the necessity of obeying His words in both of these final teachings. He really wants to make sure we understand.

In the first teaching, Jesus explains that knowledge about Him is not enough to transform your life. This is easy enough to understand: even the Devil knows God, Jesus, and the Bible, and yet the Devil is clearly not a follower of Jesus; he will not enter the kingdom of heaven.[11] The most shocking part of what Jesus says here is that doing ministry and powerful works in the name of Jesus is not enough to transform your life and bring you to eternal life with Him either! Having experiences with God, being caught up in His Spirit, casting out demons, anything we would consider mighty, exciting, emotional, or even miraculous—doing all of those these things is not enough! Wow...

Only one thing is needed: obedience. "The one who does the will of my Father" will enter the kingdom (Matthew 7:21). The first people to hear this command would rightly assume that Jesus is talking about obedience to the commands He had just finished giving, the ones found in the Sermon on the Mount. As we will see, the commands He gives in the Sermon on the Mount center upon becoming more like Him. Through this sermon, Jesus is leading us to have more of God's character, and align our lives more fully with God's heart (Matthew 5:48). Jesus makes a distinction between power, gifts, and religious knowledge, and having a heart, mind, and character that is in sync with His. Jesus warns against false disciples who proclaim God's name but never pursue a true relationship with Him. In order to have a transformational, eternal relationship with God, we need to first pursue who He is and what He is asking of us, and then regularly seek His power to obey His commands. Obedience to God is the way to transformation and proof that we have received eternal life.

In the second teaching, Jesus tells us about two men who built houses—one upon the rock, and the other upon the sand. When the storms come, the house on the rock stays strong, while the house on the sand is destroyed. What is the difference? Theoretically, each man knows how to build a house—both men hear the teaching of Jesus, know the Great Sermon, know who Jesus is, and understand what is required of them—but one man chooses to build his house the way he has been instructed to. He applies Jesus' teachings practically, and he ends up with a foundation that can withstand the storms of life. The other does not put Jesus' teaching into practical action. He does not obey, and his house is swept away by the storms. Obedience to God's Word is the foundation of our lives!

Many people say, "I don't have to do anything to get to heaven. Jesus did all the work. I am forgiven, so it doesn't matter what I do or don't do in my life." Yet it seems here that our obedience is a crucial component to living in eternity. How do we understand our obedience in light of the free gift of salvation that Jesus offers us?

You may be surprised at how much the New Testament stresses our action or inaction as a condition of eternal life.[12] But our action or inaction, our obedience or lack of obedience, never means that we are "earning" heaven. It is a biblical truth that Jesus' death on the cross is the only act that earns us eternal salvation. We are too sick with sin to ever earn or deserve a gift so precious.[13]

We can't earn our salvation. We can never do enough to receive the blessings we get right now, but we must be active in receiving the gift of salvation, and participating with God in the transformation of our lives.

Remember the seventy-billion-dollar gift? Jessica knew it existed—she believed in it and even told people about it—but she never went and got it! She never let it consume or even affect her life. If she had driven to the post office, showed her ID, and grabbed the money, would anyone think she earned the money? No. Even after thirty years of spending that seventy billion dollars, would anyone look at the thousands of actions she did with the money and think that she had earned it in the first place? No. Yet in order for her to receive the gift, it was essential for her to acquire it and integrate it into her life. We participate in receiving God's gift of grace by letting it transform our lives.

If all of us were to receive that same phone call from Bill Gates, and we all went and got our seventy billion dollars, how each of us lived with that gift would look very different. Yet, fundamentally, our lives would change significantly when our bank account changed from a few thousand dollars to seventy billion. Do we have eyes to see that life with Jesus is a greater, more valuable gift than seventy billion dollars? The commands given in the Great Sermon are the ways in which we are meant to enjoy God's gracious gift of eternal life. By obeying those commands, we allow that gift to consume and transform our lives.

If we see Jesus' commands as a burden, or as something foolish, then it is the same as rejecting the seventy-billion-dollar gift, or declaring the money is no good. If we ignore or reject the commands of Jesus, when we knock on heaven's door, Jesus will reject us; He will not know us.

Taking us back to the story of rock-man and sand-man, it seems clear that the storm Jesus is talking about is the great storm of death. The three teachings that precede our section (Matthew 7:13-14, 7:15-19, and 7:21-23) all deal with death and the final judgment of heaven and hell. There is nothing in our section that tells us Jesus is deviating from this theme. It is not just the little storms of suffering that we experience in our life that test our foundation; it is the storm of death. The houses represent our lives, and the fact that the house of sand "fell with a great crash" implies that it is never rebuilt.

Jesus is emphasizing that obedience to His words is the most important aspect of our faith lives. Jesus is not an oppressive, military commander, forcing us to do His will through guilt and manipulation; everything Jesus commands us to do is for us! His commands are full of grace; they are gifts to us that we, in our sin condition, do not deserve. His commands make us into people who can stand against the storm! Remember the health analogy from the previous chapters on sin: the commands of Jesus are simply the instructions of a good doctor so that our broken lives will be transformed into strong ones. If we don't follow the instructions, the doctor won't be affected—we will.

When I observe churches in America, I feel that we get fixated on the knowledge of God. We are consumed with studying the Bible and knowing everything we can about God. We seem to be a movement obsessed with discovering the new idea, or the new way to spin the knowledge of the Bible. God wants us to be consumed instead with obeying and experiencing Him. It is as if our churches focus on helping us study pictures of beautiful waterfalls, sunsets, and beaches; we stand around the pictures every week, seeing things we never noticed before, or pointing out small details that really make the pictures come to life. In actuality, though, true life is found *experiencing* those waterfalls, sunsets, and beaches, hearing the roar of falling water, basking in the sun, and smelling the salt in the air! We can't stop at the knowledge of God; we must live it out. We are meant to know God unto obeying Him, unto experiencing Him in all of His love and power.

LIFE IN THE CITY

JAIME IS A GOOD friend of mine. We met through coaching football at our local high school. A year ago he called me up and said, "Chris, I want to change my life; I am ready to follow Jesus." From the moment Jaime said this, he became a man hungry to understand God and obey Him.

Two months later, our church started its annual Discipleship School, an intensive journey in learning and obeying the teachings of Jesus.

Normally, someone would need to be a Christian for over a year to be accepted. However, it was clear that Jaime was on another level in his hunger to obey. So he joined the class. Everything was new to him. He was trying to shake a drug addiction, he was being introduced to a whole new way of viewing women and dating, and he was being presented with an invitation to be an ambassador of Jesus in this world.

At least twice a month during this first year, Jaime and I would have similar conversations. He would make sure he was understanding Jesus' teachings, and then he would clarify what they meant for his life. He would wrestle with the obedience point in every single conversation. Yet, by the end, he always trusted Jesus.

He began confessing his sin regularly, which helped him gain strength over his flesh. He started to build daily habits of connecting with Jesus. He started noticing the homeless and the marginalized around him, and he stopped to eat with them and pray for them.

One of the policies of the Discipleship School is that if you enter the year single, you stay single until you're done, simply to help with focus and dedication. As the year was coming to a close, he developed an attraction toward a Christian woman. Again, we were up late one evening, in my garage, talking through Jesus' heart for making disciples, and Jaime's commitment to stay single during the year. After a time of wrestling, he again obeyed and decided to not pursue dating. Because of that decision, just a few months later, Jaime was in a country in the Middle East, breaking fast with a Muslim family during Ramadan, sharing about his relationship with Jesus.

A year after making these tough discipleship decisions, Jaime was a different man. And he is now in a healthy, God-honoring relationship with this woman who also waited. As I write they have just been married, and they have both stepped into leadership in our church. He is fast becoming one of the spiritually richest people I know. He regularly receives God's gift to him and spends it! He learns and obeys. He is experiencing the great richness of the Kingdom of God. These days, instead of late-night sessions of wrestling with God's discipleship commands, our late-night conversations usually center on testimonies of God's goodness and provision, and simply being in awe at the man that Jaime sees he has become in the past few years, and the future that he sees God leading him into.

My wife Maggie is one of my spiritual heroes (and yes, I think it is pretty awesome that I get to *live* with one of my spiritual heroes!) She is a hero because her relationship with Jesus is characterized by her obedience to His commands. Maggie is not going to be the loud one in the group. She is not going to have the new, exciting vision that rallies people to her side. She leads by her steadfast courage to do what Jesus calls her to do. Maggie's parents are immigrants from China. They endured a lot of suffering in their early years and worked hard to move their family into a middle-class community. Maggie's two older brothers obtained graduate degrees and established good careers. You can probably imagine the shock they felt when Maggie told them that we were moving in a direction completely opposed to the American dream, that we were pursuing downward mobility to obey God.

Maggie's parents aren't church goers, so she could not appeal to the authority of the Bible to help ease their frustration. There were many difficult conversations that ended with lots of tension. By this point in our marriage, I had learned how important honoring parents was in the Chinese culture. After the conversations would end poorly, I would always worry about my wife, wondering how we were going to get through this. Yet, Maggie was never rattled. She displayed incredible trust in Jesus, insisting that we need to obey His call on our lives. She would remind me that the safest place to be in life is at the center of doing God's will. She kept leading us to pray. Never once did she waver, make excuses, or find some religious way to justify getting out of obeying Jesus.

Eventually her parents stopped being upset. They agreed to support us! While the initial year was full of tough conversations, I can now see after ten years how much better Maggie's relationship is with her parents because we obeyed Jesus. There is a deeper respect between them, and Maggie is so much more secure in obeying Jesus, even if it means initially that her parents will disagree. Maggie has seen this happen with decisions to have our children go through public schools, take our children to different countries to live in their poorest neighborhoods, and with our "all-in" commitment to Jesus and the building of His church. Jesus always has her back with her family when she obeys Him. She never lets the initial awkwardness or tension keep her from obeying. She is one tough, faithful, and beautiful woman! I won the lottery getting to marry her.

GOING FORWARD

MY MENTOR JOHN LO says it well: we are educated beyond our obedience. We often focus on simply *knowing* the words of Jesus instead of actively putting those words into practice in our lives. We would see so much more transformation if we gathered, talked, and prayed through just one teaching from the Great Sermon, helped each other consider how to obey that teaching, and then actually went out and did it!

As you continue to read this book and begin considering the commands given in the Great Sermon, don't rush through it. Commit to reading one chapter, studying the specific text of the Sermon on the Mount, and then living it out practically before moving on to the next command.

Obeying the words of Jesus is the only way to change our lives. The evil growing through our sin cancer wants to twist us to look toward anything for comfort and change but Jesus, and to convince us that there are many roads to new life and transformation apart from Jesus. Often, these other paths feel good in the short term, but they do not lead to lasting change. The only way to experience life-giving change is by living in obedience to Jesus. He alone gives us the correct prescription through His commands, which free us from our sin cancer and give us a rich inheritance.

Obey Jesus, and teach others to do the same. In the end, though we each will have lived very different lives, joy and transformation will come because we have become people who live out the Great Sermon.

So as you prepare to dig into the Great Sermon, stand up with new fire in your eyes. Stop making excuses that allow your sin cancer to own you and eat you up inside. Look honestly at your life and own up to your issues. Run into the arms of your heavenly Father and drink from His love. Take courage and do something. Take real steps to live out the Great Sermon in your daily life. Prepare for suffering—transformation (like surgery) can hurt. But prepare for joy and transformation to burst forth from any suffering you might endure. I say it again: stand up with new fire in your eyes. Obey and you will truly live with Jesus.

QUESTIONS TO CONSIDER

1. What do the 'riches of God' look like? Have you 'cashed in' on them?

2. How do you normally respond when obedience is hard?

3. How do you see God calling you to a life of transformation based on obedience to His Word?

---

[10] Luke 15:11-32, Ephesians 1:7-14, Philippians 3:14, Colossians 2:2-3, 2 Timothy 4:8, 1 Peter 1:4.

[11] James 2:14-19.

[12] Matthew 6:14-15, 7:1-5, 18:21-35, Mark 4:24-25, 9:42-49, 10: 17-31, Luke 6:37-38, 9:23-26, 10:25-37, 12:13-21, 14:33, 16: 10-13, John 5:14, 15:1-11, 1 Corinthians 6:9-10, Galatians 5:22-24, 6:9, Ephesians 2:10, 5:5, 1 Timothy 4:14-16, Hebrews 3:12-14, James 2:17-20, 1 John 1:6-10.

[13] Ephesians 2 is a great summary of Jesus' actions as the only actions to earn our salvation.

[14] Donald A. Hagner, *Word Biblical Commentary*, Matthew 1-13 (Dallas: Word Books Publisher, 1993), 189-191.

CHAPTER FIVE

DOWNWARD MOBILITY: BECOMING A SERVANT

"Blessed are the meek, for they will inherit the earth.
Blessed are the merciful, for they will be shown mercy.
Blessed are the peacemakers,
for they will be called children of God.
For I tell you that unless your righteousness surpasses
that of the Pharisees and the teachers of the law, you
will certainly not enter the kingdom of heaven."

- Matthew 5:5,7,9,20

"And if anyone wants to sue you and take your shirt, hand
over your coat as well. If anyone forces you to go one mile, go
with them two miles. Give to the one who asks you, and do
not turn away from the one who wants to borrow from you."

- Matthew 5:40-42

"So in everything, do to others what you would have them
do to you, for this sums up the Law and the Prophets."

- Matthew 7:12

THE DESIRE TO BE SERVED is one of our core longings. Evidence for this lies in the most common conflict between husbands and wives: both want to be served by the other.

In many homes in my neighborhood, the husband works long hours and comes home tired each day. He walks into his house, hoping that his wife will be ready not only to take to care of him, but to take care of the kids also so that he can relax in front of the TV. The wife has spent all day with the kids, dealing with bills, food, and laundry. So when she hears the door open, she is hoping her husband will play with the kids and get them ready for bed, so she can chill out in front of the TV.

When both parents are working—at home or in the office—both partners expect the other to take up the slack, do the dishes, love on the kids, and anticipate needs. In homes that are run by a single parent, there is always more to do than energy and time to do it. The need to be served is constantly felt.

Jesus explains that His standard of loving another person is determined by how we want to be loved: "So in everything, do to others what you would have them do to you, for this sums up the Law and the Prophets" (Matthew 7:12). We are to recognize our deep need to be served and then serve others in the way we desire to be served.

This does not mean that we participate in one or two big service events and call it a year. Instead, we are to work against our greedy sin cancer by regularly sacrificing for others around us.

WHAT GOD SAYS

OF ALL THE POWERFUL, counize, countercultural challenges in Jesus' Great Sermon, none creates so much tension as Matthew 5:40-42: "And if anyone wants to sue you and take your shirt, hand over your coat as well. If anyone forces you to go one mile, go with them two miles. Give to the one who asks you, and do not turn away from the one who wants to borrow from you." Jesus spoke these words to a strong Jewish people who loathed the brutal oppression of Caesar and his Roman army. Some Jewish people in the time of Jesus believed in violent rebellion (for example, Simon the Zealot, one of Jesus' original twelve disciples,[15] was associated with a group of Jews who believed in this kind of violent resistance toward Roman rule in Judea). Eventually Caesar became so tired of trying to rule this insubordinate group of people that he attempted to destroy them all.[16]

In Jesus' day, Roman soldiers flooded the streets and marketplaces of Jewish cities. By law, they were permitted to command any random person to carry something for them, up to one mile. You can imagine how shameful this would be for a Jewish person. But Jesus, who never shies away from hard truths, tells them that if they want to follow Him, they must become people who joyfully say yes to carrying something one mile, and then eagerly volunteer to go one more!

Picture this act of service: a common man, wearing casual clothes, is carrying food from the market for a Roman soldier who is riding a horse. This, by definition, is a servant. This, by definition, is the way of Jesus.

I know what may be going through your mind right now: Jesus is weak. Following Jesus is setting me up to be run over. Following Jesus is setting me up to be laughed at. But are you sure?

Stick with Jesus and trust that He, as God, knows how to give you joy better than you do. Often, Jesus challenges our instincts and quick reactions, asking us to step back and trust Him with a long-term view of change.

The end goal of Jesus' work is a complete personal, familial, social, and global revolution. He is leading a revolution. He understands the secret to true change and true power: sacrificial and servant-based love. It is the ONLY method of transforming our enemies into our advocates. The best alternative is a life spent trying to defeat enemies, which will only create new ones. Jesus offers us much more.

Be a servant to other people. Isn't this how you want other people to treat you? We experience great joy when other people take care of us. Can you imagine coming home from work and having someone give you a massage, offer you a hot meal, clean your house, take care of all your errands, and be there to absorb any annoying, frustrating problems that are in your life, every single day?

In order to be like Jesus, servanthood must become central in our character and lifestyle. There is no place, activity, or role where we are not to be servants! We are to serve in our workplace, on the basketball court, in church, and within our own households. How are you trying to be a servant to others in all places? How are you choosing to sacrifice your own interests, comforts, and desires so that others are treated well?

The environment in which Jesus gave this teaching was oppressive; fear and violence were used daily to control people. Within that environment of fear, Jesus called people to be servants. The call to servanthood is not just a call to be a nice person. It is a call to change a broken society, and it starts with small actions.

LIFE IN THE CITY

I MET CARLOS while I was coaching football in East LA. From the very beginning, coaches and players knew that I was a Christian pastor. I quickly became friends with the other coaches, as we shared the same vision of developing our football players into great men. Carlos shared this vision also, but he didn't share my Christian beliefs and lifestyle. Instead, he mocked me. Sometimes, when I approached the coaches in conversation, Carlos would be telling his crazy stories. He would stop and ask if I was judging him, or say, "Oh, we can't talk about that with the pastor here." Carlos had his reasons. He grew up in our neighborhood, saw his brother shot to death, survived being shot himself, and was suspicious of Christians. He told me, "A friend of mine found Jesus years ago, and he tried preaching to me...But you can't convert the devil."

Two years into coaching, I saw Carlos walking toward me on the field. I took a deep breath, ready for a zinger. But this time, he just walked up to me and said, "I am disgusted with my life. I need to go to your church." There was a long pause while I tried to figure out if he was being serious or setting me up. Finally, I assured him that if he came to our church he wouldn't be judged, and that he would ultimately learn how Jesus alone could transform his life. Months later, I baptized Carlos and his teenage son. Carlos became a follower of Jesus, and I walked him through the Great Sermon.

Carlos is a bus driver on one of the most traffic-congested routes in the city of Los Angeles. This means that he often deals with people at their worst, people who have their sin-natures fully activated by anger and frustration. If you don't believe me, ditch your car for one week in LA and only ride the bus! By the end of the week, you will have no doubt that you too are a sin-infested, angry, selfish person who desperately needs Jesus to live. Unfortunately, bus drivers often receive the brunt of people's frustration. Before Jesus, Carlos would deal with these frustrations the way he was taught to—the way of the streets. If somebody gave him attitude, he returned more. If somebody threatened him, he fought right back.

About three weeks into our study of the Great Sermon, as Carlos was reading Matthew 5, I got a call. I picked it up and said, "Hello." It was almost ten minutes before I said another word. Carlos was angry, shocked, and at his wit's end. "It is impossible to do what Jesus says!" he said. He started venting about the foolishness and impossibility of being a servant to the people on the bus, returning love after they dished out hate. However, by the end of his rant, he had actually convinced himself that Jesus' way was the best way. His emotions and words to me were actually one of his most genuine prayers to God—honest, raw, and humble, trying to understand his heavenly Father's heart. He realized that, in the end, the way of the streets that he had embraced for forty years was not the way to power and life. As he finished, all I said was, "Carlos, I don't think you need to hear any words from me. I'll just pray for you."

A year later, Carlos was a completely different bus driver. One day, a young woman tried to get on his bus without paying. Carlos checked her. She began to go off on him, hoping to intimidate him into letting her ride for free. She called him names, got racial with him, and gave him the whole street attitude. Carlos absorbed all of her words and began to pray for her in order to fight the anger that was welling up in his heart. He held his ground firmly, never saying a negative word to her or raising his voice. (Eventually the other riders on the bus convinced the lady to pay so that they could get going.) This lady sat down behind Carlos and continued to pepper him with insults until she got off the bus. Carlos remained silent and prayed for her.

Three days later, he pulled up at a stop, only to find his newfound enemy waiting. When she saw him, her eyes lit with fire. Carlos chose to focus on a disabled lady who was also waiting at the stop, and he helped her onto the bus. At the next stop, Carlos picked up another disabled woman who was friends with the first one. Carlos helped the two older ladies sit together in the front. As Carlos drove, he engaged the elderly women in some friendly conversation, and they began to affirm him. They talked about how handsome he was, how he was the kindest bus driver they had met, and how no other bus driver treated his riders like family. They shared stories of Carlos going the extra mile to help them.

During this conversation, Carlos kept looking at his "enemy" in his mirror. At first, he saw confusion on her face as she listened to these ladies. Eventually, the anger on her face disappeared, and she began to smile. Later in the route, when Carlos's "enemy" got off the bus, she apologized and thanked him for being such a great bus driver. Carlos no longer had an enemy; now he had another friend and advocate. How did this happen? Not only by forgiving his enemy, but also by demonstrating servanthood to two elderly ladies. Through trusting in the leadership of Jesus, Carlos changed the social atmosphere on his bus. That is the start of a healthy revolution.

GOING FORWARD

WHAT WOULD HAPPEN IF, every day when you went to work, you asked Jesus for eyes to see how you could serve your co-workers, especially those who are the most difficult to serve? What if you became known as the one who was always thoughtful, always offering to do the work that nobody else wanted to do? What would happen if servanthood was the primary DNA of churches and families?

I am so sad to see the lack of true biblical, Jesus-based, sacrificial servanthood in our church communities and families. It is easy to go the extra mile when someone is watching, when there's a chance of receiving praise, but that is not true servanthood. The true servant heart seeks to serve where there is need, regardless of the sacrifice it requires. We don't need the help of Jesus to do random acts of kindness. We don't need Jesus to volunteer for things that get us celebrated and promoted. People do nice things all the time as a way to satisfy that deep thirst of serving ourselves. But when we are living self-sacrificially, when serving someone else costs us something—our money, our time, our pride—only then do we allow Jesus to insert His scalpel and remove the cancer within us. Only then will we see transformation.

Servanthood starts at home

I BELIEVE THE BEST test of our true nature, of how well we're serving others, is how we behave at home. We're constantly trying to make a good impression outside of the home, but we drop our masks at home, where rewards and accolades are rarely given. How many people do you know who act patiently and lovingly in public, but are selfish, argumentative, defensive, and critical in their own homes?

Do you live this double life? Let me remind you: God is in your home. And who you are at home is who you truly are. To change society, we must start by changing the primary social unit—the family. We don't stop there; Jesus is not telling His disciples to hide away from the evils of their community and just obey His commands in the home. We must seek an integrated life, where obedience to the commands of Jesus is happening in all layers of society, starting with our families.

In some circles of the Christian church, husbands claim "head of the household" on a regular basis.[17] However, instead of letting Jesus and Scripture define what that looks like practically, they use it as a trump card to never serve or do the hard work at home. Husbands, if you want to be the leader in your home, you must lead like Jesus. Scripture says that Jesus, and Jesus alone, is the model of leadership. Jesus washed dirty feet (John 13). Jesus did the most difficult work so that His disciples would develop into the leaders that God made them to be.

There is no a cookie-cutter mold of what a Christian household looks like, and it's going to be difficult to continually imitate the self-sacrificial leadership of Jesus. The complex, fast-paced lifestyle that many of us lead has more demands on home life than both husband and wife can meet. We need to regularly talk with our spouses about how we act and live in our homes, so that we can keep growing into more consistent and more genuine servants there.

We should each regularly evaluate our willingness to serve others self-sacrificially by evaluating how we act within our families. It will require a big bite of humble pie, but it is living in reality. Jesus asks us to identify and acknowledge our sin rather than ignore it.

Be a servant leader

FOR ANYONE WHO is in a place of leadership in any area of our society, there is a choice: lead as the world dictates—where everyone serves the leader, or lead as Jesus dictates—where the leader serves the people being led. So for husbands, mothers, pastors, and leaders, the way to lead a family, a church, or an LA bus is to be like Jesus and lay down your life for others. Put them first.

By recognizing Jesus' example of self-sacrificial leadership, of servanthood that leads to revolutionary change in our broken society, we must realize that choosing the path of servanthood is choosing the path of greatest strength. Consider these words from the Rev. Dr. Martin Luther

King, Jr., who showed us what happens when we obey Jesus: "Far from being the pious injunction of a Utopian dreamer, the command to love one's enemy is an absolute necessity for our survival. Love even for enemies is the key to the solution of the problems of our world. Jesus is not an impractical idealist: He is the practical realist."[18]

It takes so much strength to follow Jesus into a life of servanthood, and like all kingdom living, to obey Jesus is to regularly ask Him for the strength to obey. But living like Jesus did—as a servant—also gives strength, among many other blessings. Just revisit the very first words of the Great Sermon (referred to as the Beatitudes, Matthew 5:1-12) for a reminder of all the blessings Jesus offers those who choose to be servants in this world.

You are not weak if you serve. You are living in the strength of God! Let the revolution begin.

QUESTIONS TO CONSIDER

1. Why do you think Jesus chose to present Himself as a servant, rather than a military commander, as some expected?

2. What are the costs of truly serving others, within your family and home, at work, or in your social circles?

3. What are the benefits?

---

[15] Note: This Simon is different from Simon Peter.
[16] Doug Reed, "Who Were the Zealots?" *The Crown Journal*, accessed November 29, 2016, *www.thorncrownjournal.com/timeofchrist/zealots.html*.
[17] Ephesians 5:22-33.
[18] Martin Luther King, Jr., *Strength to Love* (Minneapolis: Fortress Press, 2010), 44.

CHAPTER SIX

LOVE THOSE WHO ARE HARD TO LOVE

"Do not judge, or you too will be judged. For in the same way you judge others, you will be judged, and with the measure you use, it will be measured to you. Why do you look at the speck of sawdust in your brother's eye and pay no attention to the plank in your own eye? How can you say to your brother, 'Let me take the speck out of your eye,' when all the time there is a plank in your own eye? You hypocrite! First take the plank out of your own eye, and then you will see clearly to remove the speck from your brother's eye."

- Matthew 7:1-5

"So in everything, do to others what you would have them do to you, for this sums up the Law and the Prophets."

- Matthew 7:12

"If you love those who love you, what reward will you get? Are not even the tax collectors doing that? And if you greet only your own people, what are you doing more than others? Do not even pagans do that? Be perfect, therefore, as your heavenly Father is perfect."

- Matthew 5:46-48

DRIVING WEST ON THE 10 Freeway in my beat-up 1986 Mazda hatchback with every possession I owned, I was feeling the adrenaline pumping. It was August in Los Angeles, which meant temperatures of around one hundred degrees. Without air conditioning, I was usually cranky and drenched in sweat on a long drive, but on this particular drive, I was singing with joy.

I was moving into South LA, a hundred yards from the USC campus, ready to begin a new job as a campus minister with InterVarsity Christian Fellowship. Excited, I pulled up to the men's staff house and walked up to the front porch. What I found utterly shocked me.

It was Rocky. He was sleeping on the porch. Not taking a nap, sleeping—the porch was his home. I was expecting to meet my new boss, Jim, or perhaps a few college students hanging around. I was not expecting to see a homeless man. My first thought was that I had the wrong house. But then Jim came out the front door, stepped over Rocky, and welcomed me to my new home.

I found out later that Jim and the other pastors had been working with Rocky for a long time. At one point he was living inside the house, but after breaking some rules, he was asked to stay on the porch. He had successfully kicked his cocaine habit and was now fighting against his last addiction—alcohol.

I was deeply uncomfortable around Rocky and the entire homeless community around USC. I had never lived around the homeless and did not know how to act. I had never lived in a place where society's economic extremes so closely intersected, where you could walk a hundred yards and rub shoulders with society's most elite as well as society's most marginalized.

Feeling uncomfortable, and a little guilty, I started giving money to many of the homeless people I met. I encountered many on my walk to campus each day, and it became stressful just going to work. I quickly realized that cold cash was not helpful for those on the streets who struggled with addictions, so I began to talk to them, offering to buy food or bus tickets instead. As I listened to their stories, it was difficult to discern between truth and lies, which in turn made it difficult to maintain compassion.

After more than a year, I realized that I was being consumed by all of these interactions. I was using a lot of my energy to interact with people to and from work, while the work with students on campus became a distant second. I started getting angry—with the situation and with my inability to take control of it. All my anger culminated one day after getting scammed yet again.

I had refused to give a man cash to go "visit his family," so he asked for bus tokens. We went to the grocery store, and I bought him a monthly pass. As I left, I saw him go back into the store, return the bus pass, and use the money to buy alcohol. That was the last straw. I told myself that I was done trying to help homeless people. I began putting limits on who I cared for. I walked right by them and ignored their requests for help, convincing myself that I was here to help college students only.

Where do you draw your limit? We all have them: certain people at work, certain personality types, certain ethnicities, certain family members, even certain neighborhoods.

What about the limits on how much people can hurt us? We all have a limit as to how much we can be hurt by someone, angered by someone, or manipulated by someone before we cut them out of our lives. Who are the people you have cast out of your circle?

WHAT GOD SAYS

EVEN THOUGH JESUS covers many practical areas of life in the Great Sermon, He makes it clear what is most important to Him: *Keep Loving People.* Loving people is right at the top. In Matthew 5:43-48, He delivers another body blow to our sin-infected egos:

> "You have heard that it was said, 'Love your neighbor and hate your enemy.' But I tell you, love your enemies and pray for those who persecute you, that you may be children of your Father in heaven. He causes his sun to rise on the evil and the good, and sends rain on the righteous and the unrighteous. If you love those who love you, what reward will you get? Are not even the tax collectors doing that? And if you greet only your own people, what are you doing more than others? Do not even pagans do that? Be perfect, therefore, as your heavenly Father is perfect."

Even though society says it is okay to hate our enemies and encourages us to put limits on whom we care for, Jesus says that to follow Him and be on His team, we must blow up all the boundaries we've set.

Here we go again....Are you serious, Jesus? How is this possible?

Jesus employs a similar method in this teaching as He does in His teaching on anger and lust. He creates a spectrum—murder on one end, anger on the other; adultery on one end, lust on the other—and says we should treat every stop along the spectrum as essentially the same. In this case, one end of the spectrum holds those who are closest to us—"those who love us"—and on the other end are our enemies. Two extremes, and yet we should treat both our best friends and our enemies, and everyone in between, with love.

Think about how strong the word "enemy" is. It takes a lot for someone to become your enemy. Even the most difficult people in our lives are just that—difficult. It is rare to have another human being in our lives who is actively and passionately trying to bring pain and misery upon us (although tragically it does happen from time to time, and we need to find healthy ways to exit relationships with those few people). Jesus says that He expects us to love those people who are actively trying to hurt us! Therefore, in accordance with His teaching method, we are to love everyone else within the spectrum as well. We are to treat our *enemies* with as much love as we treat our friends. And if we are called to treat our enemies with love, then He obviously calls us to love those who simply annoy us, those who are difficult or different, and even those whose friendship would bring about what teenagers call "social suicide."

Why, Jesus? Three reasons: because God loves His enemies, because we are called to be like God, and because we are no different from evil people if we only love those who love us. Ouch!

Your sin cancer may be flaring up right now. Is it trying to convince you that there must be a loophole? Is it trying to find some sort of gray area where you can wiggle out of loving those people who are coming to your mind right now? Unfortunately, there is no loophole, and there is no gray area. One of the most difficult aspects of knowing the authentic Jesus is His straightforward, black and white, call-it-like-is approach to leading our lives. We love to get philosophical and poetic—agreeing with Jesus that African-Americans and Mexicans should unite, that immigrants and lifelong citizens should unite, but then we think that it is totally fine to justify disliking an annoying co-worker or rude neighbor. Jesus does not let us live in this kind of hypocrisy.

Remember how severe your sin cancer is. Remember how polluted you are and how often you turn your back on God. Remember how frequently you are ashamed of Jesus in public. You are not just a difficult child for God to love. At times we think and act in ways similar to God's enemies, grieving His heart. Yet He still loves you! He still loves me! We are always overwhelmed with His grace and patient love.

So how can we kick out another human being from our circle of love? If we want to be on God's team, we can't kick people out. We can't even have a circle at all.

Another reason God wants us to love those who do not love us in return is that it will distinguish us from those who do not follow Jesus. Every single person in this world loves those who love them—people who live by the rules and people who break them, poor people and rich people, people from every nation. If we live with limits on those we love, giving our best energy to those who are easy to love and who love us in return, then we are no different from those who profess that there is no God. Ouch!

There are many ways that Christians are supposed to be different from those who reject Jesus, but the New Testament makes it clear that the most foundational way we are to be unique from non-Christians is by loving people who are difficult to love. Our radical, "no limits" kind of love for our enemies should be the most visible sign to the world that we are deeply committed to following the leadership of Jesus. Most of Jesus' actions and teachings in the four gospels are focused on breaking the limits people have on loving God and loving each other; He wants us to learn to love as He loves—unconditionally and without limitation! Loving all kinds of people is how we live out our calling to be the salt and light of the earth (Matthew 5:13-16), so that people see something radically different in our lives and glorify God. As followers of Jesus, we are to be different in many ways—chief among these is not the music we listen to, the clothes we wear, what we eat or drink, our entertainment options, what we do with our Sunday mornings, or even how we vote. We are to stand out and be shockingly noticed by our love for others.

God lovingly and graciously causes the sun to rise on all His enemies. If we limit our love to certain people, we assume we have a holier standard than God. Would we be comfortable with God inconsistently picking and choosing which areas of sin He is okay with and which He won't forgive?

Following the leadership of Jesus means we must enter into persevering relationships with people who do not love us back in the same way. It means we must work toward healthier, God-honoring relationships with men and women, with people of different ethnicities, with those who live in the suburbs and with those who live in the ghettos. These are not fringe issues. Following the leadership of Jesus means we build real relationships with those who own our corporate buildings and those who clean them. We must work to create real community out of brokenness and divisions, focusing our love on those we're most resistant to love—the outcasts, the addicts, and the annoying. It's the way of Jesus.

LIFE IN THE CITY

A COUPLE OF MONTHS had passed since that last interaction at the grocery store closed my heart to the homeless around USC. I was hurrying home from campus late one night. I had recently gotten married and was in a hurry to make it home by midnight so my wife wouldn't worry—it was two minutes till midnight. There was a tall hedge lining the sidewalk and pathway leading up to my house. As I hurried around the corner of the hedge up to my house, I tripped over a homeless man sitting on my property. I freaked out. It was dark, and late, and I hate horror movies...

The man—his name was Eddie—started apologizing profusely, telling me he was so tired from walking that he just needed to rest before continuing on his journey. Before I could get a word in, he started telling me his life story: homeless, diabetic, and living in a garage until tonight when he was kicked out. He was trying to walk five miles to a family member's home to see if he could stay there until he figured something out. But with his age and diabetes, he didn't have enough energy to continue, so he stopped to rest.

I listened with a deeply skeptical heart. I knew he was telling me this sob story so that he could ask for money. I was late and didn't want to deal with any negotiations, so as soon as I could get a word in, I cut him off. "Eddie, I'm sorry for what you are going through. I need to get in my house right now, but let me get you some food so you can have some energy to get on your way." I rushed inside before he could counter. I ran right past my startled wife, mumbling, "Another homeless person." I made a sandwich, grabbed a granola bar, a piece of fruit, and a Gatorade, and went back outside. I gave it to Eddie and tried to just slide away saying, "Good luck." Eddie said, "Thank you so much, Chris. I couldn't have done this without you. You are so generous."

My curiosity got the best of me, and I stopped; I figured this was the moment he was going to ask me for money. Knowing my sin cancer, I probably wanted to stay to prove that I was right, that he was, in fact, trying to scam me into giving him money for drugs. I looked at the needle marks in Eddie's arms. Earlier, he had pointed to them explaining that they were from insulin shots, but in my head I "knew" he was lying. Eddie started telling me more of his painful life story. When he was finished, I quickly said, "Eddie, can I pray for you before I go inside?" His face brightened up, and he said, "Please!" I closed my eyes and was shocked to feel Eddie wrap his arm around me and put his head on my chest. He smelled. I had never been this close and personal with a homeless person. I prayed for him, but all the while my heart beat faster and faster. He cried while I prayed for him. As I went to say Amen, I thought, "Get ready to deny his request for money."

I said Amen and braced myself. Eddie wiped his eyes, said, "Thank you," and walked away. I couldn't believe it. He didn't ask for money! After about four steps, Eddie turned around. Okay, I grinned, here it comes. However, what happened next became one of the most special, foundational moments in my life. It was one of the few times I knew beyond a doubt that I was standing in the presence of Jesus, listening to His words. This is what Eddie said: "Chris, I can't thank you enough. Sitting here, before you came, I didn't think I could make it. I lost hope. God sent you to me in this time, like an angel. You listened to my story; you took time to make me food. You prayed for me. You believed me." He paused, and then added, "I love you, Chris." Eddie turned and walked away.

I sat down on my porch steps, paralyzed. There were so many emotions going through me. I felt guilty because I knew I was "caring" for Eddie with a twisted and negative heart. I felt the awe of being in the presence of Jesus (Matthew 25:31-46). I felt cold icicles falling off my heart. I felt the walls I had put towards the homeless come down. It all made sense in that moment. Loving those whom others will not love is a very difficult and messy process, but in the midst of messy relationships, Jesus is there. He is friends with those who have no friends. If Jesus loves them, then we must love them because we love Jesus. We must shine brighter in this dark and twisted world that only loves when it is easy. And in the end, the world will be changed. We will be blessed. We will be transformed.

We will look more like Jesus. Jesus gives us so much more joy than we can give ourselves!

GOING FORWARD

JESUS HELPS US SEE that harmony and comfort are not the signs of a great relationship. Harmony and comfort are simply the signs of an easy relationship. The ability to love and to build a relationship in the midst of differences is the sign of a great relationship. One of the first steps in being able to obey Jesus in building these kinds of Kingdom relationships is knowing who you are. We must be secure in God's love for us, and secure in our identity as forgiven children in order to persevere in difficult relationships. If we are not secure as God's precious kids, then we are looking for relationships that will make us feel secure, which will never allow us to be in relationships with people who are different from us.

As you consider the people around you who are different ethnically and racially, are you secure in who God has made you ethnically and racially? Can you articulate your culture, both the aspects of God that are found in your culture and the aspects of sin? As you consider the people around you who belong to a different social class than you, are you trying to gain the respect of those who are of a higher class than you out of insecurity? Are you looking to "help" those of a lower class out of a false sense of pride? The end goal of being in relationships with people who are different is not to "fix" them, or even get their respect. The end goal is love, and to continue the effort of building a mutually uplifting and encouraging relationship.

One of the many ways that we should stand out from those who do not follow Jesus is how we view and talk about differences. We should never use people's differences as a source of entertainment or humor in our conversation circles. We should never perpetuate gossip, cliques, and judgments. Instead we look to sacrifice our comforts, our personality styles, and our hobbies to enter into the world of those who have very different hobbies, communication patterns, sense of humor, and family traditions.

As we enter into these relationships we should expect awkwardness, messiness, and an unpredictable journey. Yet, we can also trust the commands of Jesus that we can expect a level of healing and transformation that would never be found by staying in circles of relational comfort.

When our church plant was ready to move from a car garage to our first storefront rental, we wanted a mural on the front of our new building. I began to connect with some of the taggers in the community and eventually a good-sized crew was meeting at our new place to work on a mural. It was a beautiful painting of our city, with an angel in a Los Angeles Dodgers baseball cap watching over it. During these weeks of painting, I started building friendships with them. It wasn't easy, as we didn't have a lot in common, and there were many awkward moments in the conversations. Yet over time, we were able to build genuine friendships. A month after the project, they all came to me, upset because the owner of another building in our community was going back on his word to let them use a room for a new art studio. He was being very stubborn about it and accusing them of stereotypical things, even though they weren't true. These taggers were really trying to become legitimate in their artistic work. I offered to talk to the owner, even though my tagger friends thought there wasn't any point in trying.

As I sat down with the owner of the building, I realized we had a few things in common. We were the same age and had the same educational background (although he did have much more wealth than I did!) But we were very different in how we viewed Jesus and the taggers. As I shared with him multiple stories about my very real friendships with the taggers in the crew, his shock turned into understanding. By the end of the meeting, he agreed to let them use one of his rooms for their new art studio. The taggers were now the ones shocked, and pumped! And I was in awe of God. After some difficult initial attempts at building friendships, we were now all celebrating together. Jesus knows how to deal with our sin and weaknesses. He knows how to lead us into the greater joy. Loving those who are different from us and even difficult to love brings real transformation!

QUESTIONS TO CONSIDER

1. What boundaries have you placed around your love and service in the past?

2. While we are never to allow someone to abuse us, how can you truly love those who are very demanding or hurtful, without enabling them to stay that way?

3. When have you seen or heard about boundless love transforming a person, family, or community?

CHAPTER SEVEN

UNITY: EVERYTHING IS BETTER IN COMMUNITY

"Now when Jesus saw the crowds, he went up on a mountainside and sat down. His disciples came to him, and he began to teach them. He said: 'Blessed are the poor in spirit, for theirs is the kingdom of heaven. Blessed are those who mourn, for they will be comforted. Blessed are the meek, for they will inherit the earth. Blessed are those who hunger and thirst for righteousness, for they will be filled. Blessed are the merciful, for they will be shown mercy. Blessed are the pure in heart, for they will see God. Blessed are the peacemakers, for they will be called children of God. Blessed are those who are persecuted because of righteousness, for theirs is the kingdom of heaven. Blessed are you when people insult you, persecute you and falsely say all kinds of evil against you because of me. Rejoice and be glad, because great is your reward in heaven'"

Matthew 5:1-12a

AS A YOUTH FOOTBALL coach in my community, one of the biggest challenges I face every season is building unity among my nine- and ten-year-olds. In my opinion, football is the most unselfish, team-building sport that exists. I get kids who have played basketball, soccer, and baseball.

In these sports, every kid touches the ball. Every kid gets a chance to shoot baskets, kick the soccer ball, or hit a baseball. However, in football, only about five kids on a team of thirty will ever touch the football.

The first month of every season starts in the same way. Every kid (and almost every parent) thinks they should be the quarterback or the running back. Once I choose these special positions, the great challenge is convincing the lineman that even though they can't play the position of their favorite NFL player, they are still as important as the quarterback. At some point I need to have the unity talk, where I point to the scoreboard and say, "When Jose scores a touchdown, does that scoreboard say, 'Jose 7, Visitors 0'?" They respond, "No-Sir!" and then I launch into my speech about how when one person scores, the whole team scores.

Every year I have a very diverse team. I have kids who represent at least three different racial groups, whose financial backgrounds range from difficult poverty to comfortable stability, who come from different family situations, and of course who have different personalities. Each team and kid is different in how they embrace this notion of team unity. However, the success of each season is always dependent upon how united the team becomes.

The same is true in our families and in our cities. When a household only cares about its own success, and isolates itself from the rest of the neighborhood, that city will never be able to "win" and transform in the issues of pain that plague the city. It is our unwillingness to jump into the difficult task of building unity that will keep us stuck and in a cycle of dysfunction.

Jesus' first words in the Great Sermon show us His heart for building unity with every kind of person. "The fact is, Jesus looked out over a motley crowd full of hurting people who had largely been ignored by that society and told them, 'I have some great news for you. Heaven wants you, even if nobody around here seems to.'"[19] When we consider the type of people that Jesus is handing out blessings to (poor in spirit, mourners, meek, and merciful), we have to admit that in our broken world, these are the not the type of people who get picked first. These are not the type of people who everyone is rushing to build friendships with. Yet Jesus is clear that he includes them within his relationship circle.

We see the value of unity in the blessing that a peacemaker receives—to be called a child of God (Matthew 5:9). If you want to be like your heavenly Daddy, then you work to bring unity to those who are divided. God's heart to repair broken relationships continues throughout the Great Sermon. Through His practical teaching on anger, divorce, lust, honesty, and forgiveness, Jesus shows us that building unity is a core value in His kingdom. People matter a lot, and diverse people walking together in real relationships are a visible sign that our God is transforming a broken world.

The root source of all pain and suffering in this world is spiritual, and thus relational. People die in wars because of racism, unforgiveness, and competition. People die from a lack of food because of greed and an absence of compassion. Regardless of the symptom, it originates from relational brokenness between us and God, and between us and others. As we can see in the Great Sermon,

Jesus, the great Healer, is all about relationships. He is all about leading us down a path of spiritual and relational transformation.

We all instinctively want comfort. Sin cancer inflames this natural desire and convinces us that, since some relationships can be difficult, messy, and uncomfortable, they aren't worth our time. Instead, we hang out with people who are like us because it's comfortable, and thus live no differently from atheists or secularists. As Jesus says in Matthew 5:46, even people who are devoted to corrupt living care for their friends (who are likely also devoted to evil). How can we claim that Jesus has changed our lives when our lives don't look any different from those who reject Jesus?

There is a trend I've seen in Los Angeles, that may also be happening elsewhere, away from real commitment to a geographical and church community and towards greater individuality. The cultural understanding on the streets of LA is that finding the best life is an independent one. If you can cut the strings of real commitment and be free floating, doing whatever you want, bouncing in and out of relationships whenever you want, then you'll have joy. It's become trendy to have many acquaintances, but very few people with whom you spend significant time.

At the root of this type of independence is a desire to live in comfort. It takes significant time and energy to have real relationship with people; it's messy and uncomfortable. When you have a slew of acquaintances and no deep friendships, you establish a very "low-maintenance" community; acquaintances don't require much from you, but friends do. But low-maintenance communities bring little joy because we are not truly known or loved, nor do we truly know and love others. You cannot have deep relationships if you are not willing to sacrifice your rights, opinions, and comforts to persevere with others.

WHAT GOD SAYS

ECCLESIASTES 4:12 SAYS, "Though one may be overpowered, two can defend themselves. A cord of three strands is not quickly broken." Jesus leads us back to this ancient Jewish scriptural truth, and empowers us to truly enter into real, genuine, never-give-up relationships with people. Having a core group of authentic friendships is more rewarding than only having a variety of fun experiences, or thousands of online acquaintances. Jesus says that true freedom from our cancer-infected souls is found in committing ourselves to other people's lives, both their joys and struggles, even when it requires great personal sacrifice. That is the example He left for us: self-sacrificial love. The way we talk about this in our church is with a simple phrase: "Everything is better in community."

When you read through the Great Sermon, as well as the life and teachings of Jesus, it is easy to see that building great relationships is very hard work—but it is a significant work that is worth the investment. The Great Sermon is Jesus' blueprint for making relationships work no matter how different people are from each other, or how bad the relationship seems to be. He commands us to pause our worship of Him to work things out with those close to us (5:21). He commands a level of purity and marriage commitment that demands we fight for unity with our spouse (5:27-32). He commands us to practically work to destroy the wall between the rich and the poor (6:2, 19-24). His teaching on love for our enemies is so radical that there is not division that a follower of Jesus can justify maintaining (5:38-48, 7:1-5). From the very start of the Great Sermon, when Jesus blesses and includes those society sees as weak, He makes it clear that to follow Him is to be a person who rejects judgments, revenge, and apathy towards those who are different. It means that followers of Jesus look to destroy walls that exist between men and women, people of different ethnicities, and people of different classes.

Rather than looking to maximize our independence, Jesus wants to take us into a more dependent, communal way of living.[20] I continue to learn that in everything, community is truly better.

As an example, consider how we learn from the Bible. Many people assume that the best way to learn from the Bible is to find the best teacher/preacher and have that person speak to a church group for forty minutes every week. Teaching is very important and should be a fundamental element of church, but in the early church, there was always a team of teachers![21] There was never just one person doing most of the work. In most "services," there was sufficient time for the entire congregation to hear from God and speak their insights to the group (1 Corinthians 14:26-32).

As we look at the four gospels, we see that Jesus spent most of His energy and time living with twelve guys and the small group of women who were present in his ministry and at his death and resurrection. He molded and shaped incredibly different people into a very unlikely team.

With the help of the Holy Spirit, they became an amazing force for the Gospel in the world. The ripple effects of their teamwork would touch billions (including us!), but it started with just twelve central people whom Jesus poured into constantly. We should learn from His model and create structures that help our churches use time in the Word to build a unified team among people who are very different from each other. Often, after a general Christian service, people walk out feeling connected to the pastor, but still in a superficial place with everyone else around them.

Through my experience as a pastor, I have learned that studying the Bible is always better in community. At first it is difficult to help people learn how to communicate well, how to use the right tools to read Scripture, how to listen to each other, how to understand the group's own cultural differences, and how all of that affects having a real discussion together. But the hard work pays off. However insightful and encouraging any one single preacher might be, groups who study the Bible together receive a hundred times more insight, more conviction, more zeal, and more theology by working together to understand what Jesus is saying to them.

This is just one example. Consider every practical issue that Jesus asks us to grow in throughout the Great Sermon—lust, anger, forgiveness, generosity, etc. If you and I were to commit to growing in these areas with a small group of people, we would be transformed a hundred times more than if we went off alone and had our own personal spiritual pilgrimages. Often times, when my personal prayer life is weak or when I have hit a wall with God, I will ask a trusted friend if I could pray with them early in the morning for a season of time, until I have worked out the kinks with God. It always works better than when I pray alone because *everything is better in community.*

As a high school football coach, I would watch my players lift weights and run every year to prepare for the season. The players who insisted on working out independently never, ever came into the season stronger or faster than the kids who worked together. We are created to live, work, perform, and grow in community. Overcoming addiction, making decisions, overcoming disappointment and hurt, and achieving dreams are all easier to do in community.

LIFE IN THE CITY

AS A YOUNG CHURCH, we wanted to follow the teachings of Jesus and function as a team. We needed to gather the core of the church and deepen relationships between them, as well as develop them into leaders. The core consisted of twenty-five extremely diverse people of different ethnicities, languages, and ages. Some people had their master's degrees, some college, some high school, and some without a high school diploma. Some people grew up in the church and others had only been in the church for one year. Needless to say, I was very nervous about what would transpire when we all got together.

I had asked this group to commit a lot of time together by meeting twice a month for a year, plus a weekend retreat. These meeting times were always after work. Young families were always scrambling to find babysitters so they could make the meetings, and many people showed up tired. Yet everyone made the commitment.

As we journeyed together, our differences became more apparent. Yet because of our commitment to each other, we became more comfortable talking about these differences. We were able to move past the prison of speaking only in politically correct ways, and we did not conceal our true questions and struggles, but we still sought to be honoring and respectful in the ways we shared with each other. We spoke about our racial differences, our class differences, our age differences, and our gender differences. At times there was thick tension in the room. At times there were tears. Over time we gave each other permission to "mourn" and to be "meek" with each other (Matthew 5:4-5). As people persevered in building unity, the promised blessings of Jesus were realized.

In one of our breakthrough meetings, we split the group into two: the college-educated White and Asian folks who had relocated to our city, and the mostly Latino folks who grew up in the city with a variety of educational achievements. In these two groups, we talked about what makes a great leader. When we came back together to share, the examples very different. The White and Asian group, while having some unique emphases based on cultural background, essentially agreed that a great leader was someone who was principled, full of integrity, able to model the values they taught, and able to have followers. The Latino group shared that a great leader was someone who was transparent about pain, and able to understand

and walk with others through their pain. We were amazed at how different our views of leadership were, and how both views reflected the heart of God.

Each group started to ask questions of the other about why they emphasized the things they did. At one point the room was very tense, as we realized we were not in a lot of unity about how we should lead each other and lead in the church. But as we continued talking and praying together, we experienced a sweet reconciliation.

The White and Asian folks realized that they rarely share the pain in their lives, they always assumed that it wouldn't be received as legitimate compared to the pain of their Latino brothers and sisters. As a result, they instinctively stepped into caring and support roles, which eventually turned into subtle Savior complexes. The Latino community expressed their gratefulness for the care, but asked for more intentionality and vulnerability from their Asian and White brothers and sisters in sharing their pain so as to put themselves into places where *they* needed to be led.

This resulted in the White and Asian folks intentionally going to receive prayer after church services or in small groups from the Latino community. The Latino leaders realized that they often slipped into fatalism, rooting too much of their identity in their pain. This created a wrong belief that they could never get out of a cycle of pain and overcome in such a way that they could be consistent leaders. As one Latina woman said, "I confess that when I see a Latino leader, I instinctively wonder when they will fail." The White and Asian community thanked them for modeling such vulnerability and compassion in the midst of pain and sin, but asked for the Latino leaders to step up and believe that Jesus could lead them to be consistent leaders.

There were tears and tension at points in this honest conversation and community time together, but it ended with hugs, prayer, and celebratory worship. We were becoming a church family.

At the end of the year, in our last meeting, I asked people to share how this commitment blessed their lives. One person said, "It reminded me that I often think I need personal time, but what I really need is time with community. Almost every time we had a meeting, I would be cranky. I was tired from work and family and just wanted to veg out in front of the TV. But I knew I made a commitment, and so I came. Within fifteen minutes of arriving, I was happy knowing that this was the best way I could have spent my evening."

In that last meeting, we shared stories for two hours. The previous year had been filled with lots of arguments, lots of conflict resolution and reconciliation, lots of confusion, but also lots of incredible memories of sacrificial love, learning together, deepening in friendship, experiencing the power of God, and growing as a church. Jesus had formed so much unity in the midst of so much diversity. It was a meeting I will never forget. It is a community that continues to journey together.

We can't trust our instincts and desires all the time—our sin cancer stirs up our desires for comfort—but Jesus knows us better than we know ourselves, and we can trust Him all the time. Our life is better if we commit to investing in people and walking with them, even when they are different from us.

GOING FORWARD

ONE OF THE FIRST convictions we must have is that peacemakers are needed! The most foolish thing we can do is try to ignore the many layers of division around us. The church will never lead in efforts of unity if it continues to ignore the division. To be silent and to avoid getting into the drama is to be overcome by fear. There is so much division around us because of ethnic differences, cultures, money, hobbies, personalities, gender, neighborhoods, countries, languages, and so much more. The first step is simply to be comfortable with acknowledging our differences and the divisions that those differences have caused. Then we must trust Jesus by following His lead and jumping into the mess in order to be peacemakers.

Making peace is difficult work. It is not for those who tremble in the face of anger and discontent. As followers of Jesus we are to be the world's leaders in unity, and we are to start by being honest, talking through our differences and the problems that flow from those differences. We need to regularly forgive and own up to our mistakes. We need to listen and enter into the world of those who are different from us, as learners, not as naysayers or critics. Followers of Jesus should always have their radar tuned to those who are being marginalized or feel they don't belong, and they should work to bring unity from the great amount of painful disconnect and disunity that is in our world.

Followers of Jesus are to be unity builders, reconcilers, and peacemakers. As we see in Jesus' life, there will be suffering as we step into the mess. Yet in the midst of that mess, we find great joy and receive the greatest honor, the honor of being children of God, ambassadors of our Daddy's kingdom (Matthew 5:9).

QUESTIONS TO CONSIDER

1. On my youth football team, teaching the athletes to recognize each touchdown as a team-wide victory is a process. How do you feel when someone else on your team gets a victory?

2. Does your church or community face divisions along the lines of race, class, gender, life experience, and other factors? How can you address them together?

3. What practical steps can you take to become more of a peacemaker?

---

[19] Blake Coffee, "Are You There for The Wounded?" *Christian Unity Ministries*, October 13, 2009, accessed November 26, 2016, *www.christianunityministries. org/2009/10/13/are-you-there-for-the-wounded/*.

[20] See Acts 2:42-47, in which the first followers of Jesus have given us a great example of commitment to community.

[21] All the apostles in the first church were teachers (Acts 2:42), and all elders in the churches that Paul planted were required to teach (1 Timothy 3:2, Titus 1:9).

CHAPTER EIGHT

CONFLICT RESOLUTION

*"You have heard that it was said to the people long
ago, 'You shall not murder, and anyone who murders
will be subject to judgment.' But I tell you that anyone
who is angry with a brother or sister will be subject
to judgment. Again, anyone who says to a brother or
sister, 'Raca,' is answerable to the court. And anyone who
says, 'You fool!' will be in danger of the fire of hell."*

*"Therefore, if you are offering your gift at the altar and there
remember that your brother or sister has something against
you, leave your gift there in front of the altar. First go and
be reconciled to them; then come and offer your gift."*

- Matthew 5:21-24

I HATE CONFLICT. There are few things that produce more
stomach acid than impending conflict. I have always
been a harmony guy. I want everyone to feel good in the
room. I will instinctively absorb and ignore stuff that
bothers me so that tension can be avoided.

You can imagine my horror after reading this teaching for the first time. Everything in me wanted to find
ways to ignore this particular teaching, but the grand

implication of Jesus' words didn't allow me to. I was cut to the heart by this truth: *we can't have a real and right relationship with God unless we have a real and right relationship with each other.* We can't say we are tight with God and hold grudges against others. We can't say we love God and avoid patching things up with others.

WHAT GOD SAYS

JESUS SAYS THAT if we desire to worship Him, but there is a relationship that is currently broken, then to *actually worship God is to go and work things out in that relationship.* We can't separate our relationship with God and our relationships with people. God lives in people. The very first chapter of the Bible teaches us the rock solid truth that every single person is made in the image of God.[22] Thus, to deepen our intimacy with God is to deepen our intimacy with each other. The way we deepen our intimacy with each other is by living honestly and actively working out conflict.

In order to understand the importance of reconciliation, it is helpful to realize that God's image and presence is with all human beings. Even those who would be considered enemies of God, still are made in His image and carry His presence and blessings (even if they don't acknowledge it).[23] For those who are Christian, God actually lives within us![24] When we are angry with a friend, our anger is also directed at God. When we hurt another human, we are hurting Jesus; we are hurting God's child.[25] To gossip about someone, and then to go to church and sing songs to God is not in line with God's desire—as James says, sweet praise of God and foul words about another person can't come out of the same mouth! We must choose.[26]

In our sinful hearts, we can quickly demonize people. We often put people in our little judgment prisons and throw away the key. When someone gets upset with us, our instinct is to put up our fists and fight back. Or we drift away and look for other people to hang with. In this teaching, Jesus challenges these broken reactions. He is telling us that if we want to hang with Him, we need to work out our problems with people and stop doing what everyone else does when relationships get hard. Live differently! No more fight or flight—we must engage and resolve instead.

LIFE IN THE CITY

I HAVE ALWAYS BEEN one to "fly." If things started getting awkward in a friendship, I slowly drifted away and started new friendships. There is very little drama, but also very little depth.

Eleven years ago, I was sitting in my garage with my boss, who was also my ministry partner. I was a few months away from leaving the work at USC to move into East LA, so we started reminiscing about all the great memories from our time together at USC. Then at one point, he looked me straight in the eye and said, "Chris, I want us to have a clean slate as you leave. Is there anything that you need to talk through with me? Has there been any time I have hurt you, or sinned against you?"

He and I had been working together for five years. He is one of the best supervisors I have ever had. He is one of my closest friends, the godfather of my oldest son, and a man whom I desire to emulate in many ways.

But after five years of working together, there had been moments when I was frustrated or angry with him or his leadership. The problem was that I had never brought up those frustrations in the moment. I had ignored Jesus' teaching, suppressed my anger, and tried to move on. His questions drilled into my soul, and he could tell I had issues to resolve.

My first comment was, "I feel embarrassed that I've never brought this up to you. I feel embarrassed that there are things from three years ago that I've never mentioned..." I talked through my issues. He wasn't able to even remember all of what I was bringing up. But in being like Jesus, he was gracious with me, apologized, and also forgave me for my immaturity for not bringing things up. I walked away from that conversation with a deep conviction about regularly reconciling with others.

As I entered into a new staff team at the church in East LA, I was determined to fully live out this teaching of Jesus. Anytime I thought someone had a beef with me or I felt frustrated with someone, I would initiate a conversation to resolve such issues. For a while, it was very awkward and very messy. I was not good at conflict resolution, having had very little practice. Eventually, I developed a reputation around the church. Everyone became ready for the six dreaded words out of my mouth, "Hey, could I talk to you?"

After two years of actively obeying this teaching of Jesus I was asked to teach on conflict resolution at our church. This started a new role for me in my leadership. I was called on to mediate conflict—me, the guy who used to run from the first hint of conflict. I am still not perfect in my ability and willingness to work out conflict in healthy ways, but I am actively working on obeying this teaching of Jesus. This has resulted in more honest and healthier relationships. Obedience to Jesus, which feels difficult, produces incredible transformation in our lives.

It is so crucial that leaders model a willingness to grow in doing conflict well, and a willingness to persevere in reconciliation. I am amazed to see a new "culture" of conflict resolution active in our small church. Folks who grew up with a fight or flight approach when things got bad are now sitting down with a mutual friend as a mediator, and working to get to the point where both can apologize and forgive.

There have been times when in the middle of our opening worship, I see someone cross to the other side of the room, pull a friend aside, work things out, and then end up worshipping God together. I always start to tear up knowing that years ago they probably would have been throwing punches! Just as bitterness and holding grudges can spread poison through a community, so too can courageous decisions to work out conflict and restore relationships.

GOING FORWARD

A FEW PRACTICAL TIPS are helpful when it comes to conflict resolution.

Conflict is to be expected

NORMAL, HEALTHY friendships regularly have small doses of tension, hurt, and problems. You will probably be frustrated or annoyed with a friend, or you will frustrate or annoy them. Expectations will not be met, and miscommunication will happen. This is normal! So it should become the new normal to regularly work out these issues in healthy ways. Be open to working out not only conflicts caused by getting hurt or offended, but also conflicts that begin when you hurt others. It will happen—you're human!

Sweat the small stuff

BRING UP EVEN the small issues, especially in your closest relationships. We often hear it said that you should pick your battles and only talk through the really damaging actions in a friendship. I don't agree. While we should work to give friends the benefit of the doubt and not be overly sensitive, it is often the case that big, damaging issues happen because the little ones haven't been dealt with.

When we ignore small issues, we build up resentment, and even little hurts begin to cause big reactions. My most common intro in a conflict resolution conversation is, "This is not a big deal, a two on a scale of one to ten. I am only bringing it up to work through it quickly because I don't want to have any junk stored up between us. This friendship means a lot to me." Resolve small things when they happen; it will build trust and a greater capacity for grace and understanding. As the Proverbs say, "Better is open rebuke than hidden love. Wounds from a friend can be trusted, but an enemy multiplies kisses."[27]

Start with prayer

TAKE YOUR ANGER to God before you have the conversation. Anger should be our most mistrusted emotion, and as such, we should never react in anger.[28] It blinds us to what is true, which prevents us from being able to really work through the problem with someone else. Learn how to be honest and raw with God in the midst of your anger. Vent your anger to Him, but then also talk through *why you are angry* and what is causing the anger.

Working through our emotions with God helps us get to the root of the issue and makes us more grounded for the conversation. It helps us enter the conversation with more humility, ready to truly listen to the other person, and apologize if we had a part in the conflict.

Forgiveness is the goal

THE GOAL IN TALKING with someone about how they hurt you is always to arrive at a place of forgiveness. The goal should never be winning the fight. If the goal is to win, you will end up losing the relationship. Enter the conversation determined to be honest, prepared to be messy, and committed to persevere until true forgiveness is reached. We learn what true forgiveness is through God's example: when God forgives you, He decides to never use your mistakes against you and is happy to be in right relationship with you. This is how you should forgive your friend.

Consider having a mediator

DON'T BE AFRAID to ask someone to mediate. Jesus encourages mediation in Matthew 18:15-20. Defensiveness arises in conflict resolution because we feel we need to "win"; owning up to our mistakes and apologizing often feels like we are losing power somehow. This is one reason why, in difficult conflicts, it can be helpful to have a trustworthy person sit between two people, hear them present their cases, and guide them towards listening to each other, owning up to their mistakes, apologizing, and ultimately forgiving each other. It is not shameful or weak to ask for mediation. Asking for mediation displays a passion to trust Jesus, obey His commands, and treasure reconciliation above division.

Be explicit with apologies and forgiveness

ALWAYS SPEAK THE words, "Forgive me," or "I am sorry," and "I forgive you." If the words aren't spoken, people will often walk away with a lingering doubt that everything is worked out. It is easy to feel awkward when saying these important phrases. I am convinced, because it is so hard for us to say these words, that they carry spiritual power. They carry the kingdom power of humility and self-sacrificial love. They pierce through pride, defensiveness, and a sick heart that is bent on self-survival.

When the other person is not ready

WE CAN'T FORCE someone to reconcile with us, but we can pray that God will move their hearts toward reconciliation. *True* reconciliation can only happen if both people are willing to work everything out; we can't be in real relationship with someone who will not own up to their mistakes. But we can take our pain to God and truly forgive the other person so that we can continue forward with our hearts ready to embrace them the moment they reach out in repentance. We don't have to wait for the other person to own up to their mistakes in order to forgive them.

When boundaries may be necessary

LASTLY, THERE ARE people who are so broken and so consumed by sin, that they are unable to be in real relationship. If the person is unwilling and incapable of reconciliation, then we are to forgive them in our hearts and move on, drawing healthy boundaries. Yet even if we need to put boundaries in place, we can never justify gossip or negative talk about them. Jesus is clear that we will be judged as we judge, regardless of what someone has done to us.[29] Don't be quick to decide when to move on. Remember that God has not moved on from you. When you think this may be the case, talk to a trusted friend and ask them for an objective opinion.

QUESTIONS TO CONSIDER

1. Do you tend to move toward conflict, or away from it?

2. Have you ever won (or lost) an argument, only to lose a friend?

3. What does true conflict resolution look like? How do people relate to each other after a conflict is resolved?

---

[22] Genesis 1:26
[23] Matthew 5:45-48
[24] John 15:1-10
[25] Matthew 25:31-46, Luke 15:11-31
[26] James 3:9-12
[27] Proverbs 27:5-6
[28] Matthew 5:22
[29] Matthew 7:1-5

CHAP

FORG

"For if you forgive other people when they sin
against you, your heavenly Father will also
forgive you. But if you do not forgive others their
sins, your Father will not forgive your sins."

- Matthew 6:14-15

FORGIVENESS MIGHT BE THE most complicated and difficult aspect of Christianity. And yet without it, we have no hope of living a joy-filled life. Generally speaking, we perceive ourselves as much better people than we are, much less in need of God's forgiveness than is true. This distorted self-perception makes us quicker to judge and less likely to forgive. If we have a hard time forgiving people, we need to run to God for a good dose of humility, a reality check, and a softening of our sick hearts.

Putting limits on who you will forgive ultimately hurts you. Jesus doesn't command us to forgive because He wants to make us miserable. He is the great doctor, asking us to trust Him with a life-saving surgery. It will be painful for a time, but in the end, we will finally be healthy. The very best medicine for our sin cancer is

forgiveness from God and extend for-
others. Few things give us life the way that
ess can.

WHAT GOD SAYS

FORGIVENESS IS ONE of the dominant themes in the Great Sermon.[30] Forgiveness is woven throughout—from praying for our enemies, to reconciling with people, to not judging others. But then, just in case we missed it, Jesus speaks about forgiveness directly: "For if you forgive other people when they sin against you, your heavenly Father will also forgive you. But if you do not forgive others their sins, your Father will not forgive your sins" (Matthew 6:14-15). Another way to say it is that if you forgive other people when they hurt you, God will forgive you for hurting Him. But if you don't forgive other people, God won't forgive you. Grace is free. Grace is unearned. Grace is conditional.

Forgiveness from God is conditional on us forgiving others. How? Why? I thought grace was a free gift?! Evidently, Jesus' original disciples also had a hard time with this one. So Jesus gives them, and us, more help through the parable in Matthew 18:21-35. I will let you study that on your own, but my summary of the conditional aspect of forgiveness is this: there is no way another human being can sin against you that you have not already done and will continue to do against God. Thus, we are hypocrites to ask God for forgiveness when we will not forgive each other.

It comes back to our sin cancer: if we do not rightly understand how selfish, blind, and sick our souls are, we won't understand Jesus' command to forgive all people all the time. If we can't see how severe our rejection of God has been, and how much we continue to reject Him, we won't obey the command to forgive.

To help us get some perspective, I want you to imagine standing in the middle of a huge beach, one that seems never-ending. In your hand is a bucket of sand. Think of the most hurtful thing anyone has ever done to you—the sand in your bucket represents whatever that is. Now look at the rest of the sand on the beach—that sand represents all the ways that you have hurt and dishonored God, rejected Him, worked against Him, been ashamed of Him, and been embarrassed of Him. Your sin cancer is as never-ending as the sand on that beach.

It works like this: When we get in touch with how nasty our sin cancer is, there should be a great revulsion towards our sinfulness. In the midst of this, God comes to forgive. It doesn't make sense and it makes us uncomfortable, but in the end, forgiveness is the greatest liberator. Sin, and the guilt it produces, is like a prison, and God's forgiveness sets us free. Forgiveness unshackles the chains that bind us to sin. Receiving that kind of unearned, illogical forgiveness fills our tank of forgiveness to overflowing. Then, once we have received that overwhelming forgiveness, the ways that people have hurt us aren't such a big deal. This is because we have been forgiven in such massive ways, that we are able to forgive others as well.

LIFE IN THE CITY

ONE OF MY FRIENDS grew up in a difficult neighborhood. His father died when he was very young, which kept him and his family stuck in government housing, or the "projects" as they're referred to here. He could tell you many stories of almost dying, or almost being locked away for a long time. He was a young boy without any direction or leadership from his father. The most difficult period for him was when his mother lost custody of him and his siblings for a few years, and he bounced around foster care. He was filled up with anger and hopelessness, wondering if he would make it past the age of twenty-five.

Well, that same year, at age twenty-five, he gave his life to Jesus and started to plan for his wedding. The wedding planning caused him to research the death of his father. He was always told that his father, who drove a taxi cab, was the victim of a senseless murder. You can imagine the shock when he found out that his dad smuggled drugs and his murder was linked to this lifestyle. A lot of anger filled his heart, as he realized that much of the pain that he experienced as a boy was the result of his father choosing to live an illegal life. I walked with him through this process of discovery, anger, and forgiveness. I was amazed to see Jesus help him forgive his father in such a genuine and deep way. It wasn't easy, and it was messy, but the result was miraculous.

He is now the head basketball coach at our local high school, a leader in our teen ministry, and the adoptive father of his nephew. His life is all about being a father figure to young men who are going through what he went through. And instead of bitterness towards his father causing him to act out in dysfunctional ways, he is an incredible husband: consistent, thoughtful, and generous with his wife. As I write, he is about five months from holding his first biological child in his arms and becoming the kind of father his father was unable to be for him. How was he able to break the cycle of inconsistency and anger in his family? By forgiveness, the most powerful transforming agent in our world.

He won't be a perfect father. He will make mistakes. When his kids enter adulthood, they will likely have some of the same difficult choices before them as he had. But when they understand the beaches of sand that their Heavenly Father has forgiven them, and when they understand the bucket of sin their father forgave their grandfather, I hope they will see the little cup of sin from their father, and I hope they will choose to forgive, and live in the forgiveness that now characterizes their family.

GOING FORWARD

RECEIVING FORGIVENESS FROM our Heavenly Father enables us to forgive those who have hurt us. Jesus gives us this conditional statement about grace because you can't have one without the other. They work together, like a great circular flow. We receive forgiveness, and then we give forgiveness.

Forgiveness is not a natural act. The ability to receive forgiveness from God, and to extend forgiveness to others, is supernatural. Only God can move us into this life-giving, soul-healing place, which is why He teaches us in the Great Sermon to pray this way:

> Our Father in heaven,
> hallowed be your name,
> your kingdom come,
> your will be done,
> > on earth as it is in heaven.
> Give us today our daily bread.
> **And forgive us our debts,**
> > **as we also have forgiven our debtors.**
> And lead us not into temptation,
> > but deliver us from the evil one. (Matthew 6:9-13)

Asking for help to receive and extend grace daily is as necessary as asking for food. Forgiveness is a foundational pillar of following Jesus. We are the world's only hope in this arena, as Jesus is the only one who can lead us into enduring and complete forgiveness. We should be the world's leaders in conflict resolution, not the ones contributing to new conflicts or keeping division alive.

Consider the power of forgiveness as shown by Martin Luther King, Jr. and Desmond Tutu. Powerful transformation came about because they brought the forgiveness of Jesus into the midst of great hatred. We're called to step into that kind of power in our families and churches, at our workplaces and in our neighborhoods! If there is ever an area that followers of Jesus are to shine, it is in the area of forgiveness and reconciliation. For the sake of your life, and for the sake of the world, never stop receiving and extending forgiveness.

QUESTIONS TO CONSIDER

1. What's hard about forgiving others?

2. What's hard about accepting forgiveness from God or from other people?

3. Whom do you need to forgive?

[30] Matthew 5:7, 5:23-24, 5:44, 6:12, 7:1-5, 7:12.

CHAPTER TEN

SLAYING THE GIANTS, PART ONE
OVERCOMING THE LOVE OF MONEY THROUGH GENEROSITY

"Be careful not to practice your righteousness in front of others to be seen by them. If you do, you will have no reward from your Father in heaven."

"So when you give to the needy, do not announce it with trumpets, as the hypocrites do in the synagogues and on the streets, to be honored by others. Truly I tell you, they have received their reward in full. But when you give to the needy, do not let your left hand know what your right hand is doing, so that your giving may be in secret. Then your Father, who sees what is done in secret, will reward you."

- Matthew 6:1-4

"Do not store up for yourselves treasures on earth, where moths and vermin destroy, and where thieves break in and steal. But store up for yourselves treasures in heaven, where moths and vermin do not destroy, and where thieves do not break in and steal. For where your treasure is, there your heart will be also."

"The eye is the lamp of the body. If your eyes are healthy, your whole body will be full of light. But if your eyes are

unhealthy, your whole body will be full of darkness. If then the light within you is darkness, how great is that darkness!"

"No one can serve two masters. Either you will hate the one and love the other, or you will be devoted to the one and despise the other. You cannot serve both God and money."

- Matthew 6:19-24

JESUS IS NOT SUBTLE about eternal life. He is not cryptic or mystical or overly academic. He does not try to manipulate. He says it very plainly: Do not store up treasure on earth where it will decay and where people will steal it. Do invest in the one thing that will last forever: treasure in heaven, earned by generosity on earth. When we give away our resources here, we are given eternal rewards (Matthew 6:4).

Jesus is saying, "I want you to be as rich as you can be!" Be rich in God! Jesus, the source of all wisdom, is presenting us His eternal economic plan, His prescription for building a heavenly portfolio that will last forever.

Have you ever driven through rich neighborhoods and thought, "Dang, I would love to have that house"? Have you ever seen someone pull out a wad of bills and purchase things freely, and thought, "Man, I would love to have that kind of money"? Have you ever played Monopoly and earned wads of those orange five-hundred-dollar bills by buying up all the prime real estate, wishing it were real?

While these desires are misdirected towards material possessions that won't last, Jesus' basic assumption behind this teaching is that the desire to obtain great treasure is a good thing, something that reflects your Creator's heart. The questions we need to wrestle with are: Are we seeking earthly treasure or heavenly treasure? Are we making decisions that will fulfill this desire for lasting treasure? In this teaching, Jesus assumes that our desire for treasure is a good thing, and He wants to help us get the best and most of it. Money and possessions are a poor substitute for the treasures of God.

WHAT GOD SAYS

WHEN IT COMES to our desire for wealth and treasure, how are we to get the best? Jesus is very clear on this one: Do not let your heart's desire for wealth and treasure be channeled toward temporary stuff. Money, homes, cars, clothing, gadgets, purses, food, entertainment—these things are all temporary. Instead, quench the thirst found in your heart by investing in the things that are eternal, by investing in things that will last!

Jesus' teaching on how we should pursue and handle wealth does not stress sacrifice as the ultimate goal— although sacrifice will be required. Jesus' ultimate goal for our wealth is that we would get the very best. Fundamental in His teaching is the call to be wise in our decisions, rather than foolish.

So how do we store up treasure in heaven? How do we invest in things that are eternal? It is obvious from the Great Sermon, as well as the rest of the Bible, that the only two things that are eternal are God and people! The Great Sermon shows us that in order to invest in our relationship with God, to really love Him, we need to invest in each other by loving each other. In Wall Street terms, buying shares in the kingdom of God means investing in people.

We need to accept the invitation to partner with God in sacrificially loving, blessing, and giving life to people! We are promised eternal rewards, or earnings, for doing so!

We often hear people say, "Don't trust in money and stuff because you can't take it with you when you die."[31] But Jesus is telling us that we can take it with us. We just need to smuggle it in through people! I want to be transformed by this teaching. I want to actually live in a way that shows I believe that God and people are the only two things worth investing my money in. Jesus gives a very straightforward word in Matthew 6:24 that should check all of us: "You cannot serve God and money."

In this verse, Jesus portrays money as a rival to God. He is saying that we better get serious about how we deal with money and stuff, because it has the power to take us away from God. It has the power to consume us. It has the power to decide our eternal fate. Money and temporary treasure is no casual deal. We can't separate our spiritual life with God from our practical life with money. *"For where your treasure is, there your heart will be also."* How we deal with our stuff and money reveals who—or what—we truly worship. For example, do we spend as much time budgeting our finances to live simpler and give more as we do in researching the newest thing we want to buy for ourselves?

I have heard many Christians say, "God knows my heart, and money is not first. If He asks me to give, He knows that I will." Yet these same people work very hard to build up large savings accounts, and they spend more time researching great deals on new cars, gadgets, and clothes than they do on greater giving commitments to help those in need. The intention of giving is there, but the action is lost in slavery to our sin cancer and its obsession with temporary treasure.

Remember this: a decision to follow Jesus is not just about changing our intentions—Jesus is not a God of good intentions. Following Jesus is a change of actual living— Jesus is a God of action. Saying the right thing doesn't get us to heaven. Our hearts are judged by our actions, and Jesus says our hearts are found where our treasure is.

One of the fundamental ways that followers of Jesus are to shine as lights in this world (Matthew 5:14-16) is through counter-cultural generosity, a lifestyle that demonstrates our investment in only two things: God and people. It comes down to humility and a heart transformed by Jesus. Where our treasure is, there our heart is also.

LIFE IN THE CITY

ROSA IS AN AMAZING woman. She is a Mexican immigrant who lives in a six-hundred-square-foot apartment with her husband and two kids. Every month, after they pay their rent, they live off of three hundred dollars. By American standards, they are poor. Yet you would never know it being around them. Their family lives in a spirit of joy and generosity. They always show up to church with a wonderful potluck dish, regularly volunteer for any service function, and always give some of their three hundred dollars to the work of our church.

For months, Rosa's husband Jose worked extra shifts to save money so he could host a hundred people at his daughter's birthday party. He never once complained about it. One evening, Rosa introduced her cousin to me: she had recently lost her housing and moved her family into Rosa and Jose's home until they were able to get their own place. Two families living in a six-hundred-square-foot apartment!

As I got to know them, I realized that their joy and generosity were rooted in multiple stories of Jesus providing for them. Their generosity with very little is the result of a deep faith and trust in Jesus that He will always take care of their basic needs. Years ago, when they started following Jesus, they decided to trust His teachings and began to slowly give a little of their earnings. They were amazed at how Jesus not only provided financially, but provided a deeper joy as they gave. These early moments of provision cemented in them a trust of Jesus that has resulted in their hearts being free of anxiety. They are convinced that being generous with even the little they have is the best way to live. They are living for eternity, and I can't wait to see the house that Jesus has for them on the other side.

When I read Jesus' teaching on generosity, I picture Jose, Rosa, and their children. They understand Jesus in ways that I want to. They are rich in eternal treasure. Rosa and Jose are not rich in money or possessions, but they are rich in generosity, love, hope, and faith. They live in contentment. They show me a new way of living.

GOING FORWARD

IF WE OWN UP to the sin cancer that influences our practical use and misuse of money, then we can start making changes in our life. I have found that discipline and accountability are needed until my heart gets to a place where it desires the life that Jesus offers through obedience to His teaching.

Here are some lifestyle changes that I have found helpful to begin the long, tough, rewarding journey of stripping our hearts away from the god of money, and ultimately toward the worship of our Heavenly Father.

Start with a plan

SET UP A BUDGET that is not based on what you can afford, but based only on what you actually need. (You may need help from trusted friends in determining this. We have a funny way of justifying superficial things as "essential needs"!) Then stick to your budget! Get whatever kind of help you need to do so.

Determine how much you want to give away from every paycheck, and set that money aside when you receive it. To be generous, we must make giving our first priority. Waiting to see what's left over at the end of the month shows that our heart is not yet in agreement with Jesus' teaching.[32]

Put discipline on your spending

SET ASIDE HOW much money you want to use for the month on spending habits (Target, Starbucks, McDonalds, discount stores, etc.), and once you've used up that cash, wait until next month. Many people create real or virtual envelopes that divides their money into these categories to control spending. Do not be an impulsive buyer. Remember that you don't actually need most of the things you feel you need right now—that's American consumerism talking! It requires discipline to submit to a budget, but it is slavery to submit to American materialism.

The basis for purchasing stuff should be, "Do I need it?" not "Can I afford it?" or "But it's a great deal!" People who spend their time shopping for great deals are just as consumed with temporary treasure as people who spend flippantly. A great habit to practice is praying before making a purchase.

If you are going into debt in order to obtain more things, your heart may be worshiping money and stuff instead of God. Credit card debt is a tangible sign that you are not living contentedly, that Jesus is not enough for you. If you are struggling with credit card debt, ask people you trust to help you work through the addiction. Jesus is better!

Simplify your closet

ONE PRACTICAL STEP that has really helped our family is to "give what you get." We cleaned out our closets and determined what amount of clothes was sufficient for each of us, then we gave away all the excess. Now, every time we receive new clothes at Christmas, birthdays, or from our own shopping, we trade in one old item for each new one. This kind of discipline can be done with all the stuff we have. It is spiritually healthy to regularly take inventory of our stuff, simplify, and then implement disciplines to avoid excessive hoarding. Managing physical stuff is spiritual work. Basically, do whatever it takes to cut the ties you have to material possessions. Kill that sin cancer.

Befriend those who have very little

WE ARE FRAGILE PEOPLE and are easily influenced. When we spend most of our days around people with similar resources, or even more resources, we become numb to the words of Jesus, thinking this or that level of wealth is the norm. We start living in a false reality. I am convinced that one reason why Americans are so driven and not very happy is because we are constantly looking up and believing lies that we need more, instead of looking down and realizing we actually have more we can give.

For a shock to your system, go to *www.globalrichlist.com* and type in your yearly income. You will see that even as a college student, or someone who lives in the American ghettos, you and I are incredibly wealthy. When we regularly make choices to be around those who have very little, the scales come off of our eyes and we can finally see that people and God are the only things worth investing in.

I now understand why Jesus spends so much time teaching us that those who have resources should pursue real relationships with those who don't have resources.[33] This is one of the dominant themes in all the Gospels, especially the Gospel of Luke. The book of Acts shows that a priority in the first church was building relationships with the marginalized. We are to share our wealth with those who have very little, but we also need to see Jesus in the poor for the sake of our sick souls. We need a reality check to counteract the lie that this life is about getting more and more stuff.

Avoid rationalizing away your decisions not to give

SCRIPTURE COMPELS us to give: to the church we are committed to, to missionaries, spontaneously to those in need, and toward efforts to alleviate poverty, including through our taxes.[34] But our sin cancer is nasty when it comes to giving. We have trained our minds to rationalize why we shouldn't give. For example, we might say, "If I give to a homeless person, they will use my money to buy alcohol or drugs." It is true that we should seek to be wise with our giving and never willingly enable someone to hurt themselves, but this does not mean we cannot be generous in meeting practical needs.

Another rationalization we make is that our churches and non-profits don't use the money they are given correctly. I think it is right and necessary to keep organizations in check and be wise about where we give. But we should take the time to find organizations who are using their money—our donated money—in ways that support the kingdom. And we should critique our own use of money by that same standard!

Talk about money in your communities

THERE WILL BE some people in our communities who have access to more resources, and some who have access to less. We must be content, always thankful for what Jesus provides. We must be humble, always asking Jesus for help in managing His stuff.

On the other hand, it is also spiritually harmful to create Christian communities where we never talk about money management, where we never encourage each other to pursue simpler, more generous lives. If money is one of our greatest stumbling blocks, and one of the few areas of sin that can actually compete for our worship, then we should constantly be helping each other!

Community is the best place to help each other trust Jesus. With a small circle of friends, research a great giving opportunity and be generous together. The giving impact will be greater because you are pooling your money, but it will also create a safe way to start talking about money management and Jesus' leadership in this area with others.

I do not offer these practical suggestions to create a set of rules. I offer them to help us move past a "private" Christianity, filled with good intentions, into obedience by making practical lifestyle changes that show we actually trust Jesus. But I have also learned that one of the worst things we can do in Christian community is critique each other on the small decisions we make with our money and stuff. We must stay humble, continually focusing on the log in our own eye. As soon as we start to judge our brother and sister in the area of money, we will be judged in the same area.

Someone else may have different practical disciplines they have submitted to when striving to live more simply. God will not judge between the two of us because of our different practical lifestyles. But as we learned in chapter four with rock-man and sand-man, God will judge between those who only agree with His teaching with words, and those who actually obey Jesus' words in a practical sense.

When it comes to a big area of life like money management, we must start small. Consider one or two changes you can make today that will practically help you pursue the eternal treasure Jesus offers. Understand that the journey of walking away from temporary stuff to invest in God and people may always be a struggle. Don't be afraid to get practical; Jesus walks with you.

QUESTIONS TO CONSIDER

1. Who in your life has modeled generosity to you?

2. When you think about becoming a more generous person, what thoughts and feelings come up? Are you excited? Scared?

3. What's your "investment plan" in the Kingdom of God? What practical suggestion in this chapter can you commit to today?

---

[31] Matthew 5:7, 5:23-24, 5:44, 6:12, 7:1-5, 7:12.

[32] For a deeper study on how to manage your resources to maximize giving, see Josh Lawson, *Realign: Finding God's Purpose for Your Money* (Brentwood, TN: Clear Day Publishing, 2014).

[33] To understand more how to pursue healthy relationships with the poor, see Derek Enghdahl, *The Great Chasm: How to Stop Our Wealth from Separating Us from the Poor and God* (Pomona, CA: Servant Partners Press, 2015).

[34] Luke 20:24-26, Luke 19:8-9, Luke 8:3, Acts 4:32-37, 1 Corinthians 9:14, Philippians 4:14-19.

CHAPTER ELEVEN

SLAYING THE GIANTS, PART TWO
OVERCOMING ANGER

*"You have heard that it was said to the people long
ago, 'You shall not murder, and anyone who murders
will be subject to judgment.' But I tell you that anyone
who is angry with a brother or sister will be subject
to judgment. Again, anyone who says to a brother or
sister, 'Raca,' is answerable to the court. And anyone who
says, 'You fool!' will be in danger of the fire of hell."*

- Matthew 5:21-22

I RECENTLY ATTENDED an incredible wedding in our community. It was a small gathering in the heart of the city, but filled with joy and celebration. The mariachi band kicked off the wedding, the birria (Mexican marinated beef) filled the reception hall with great smells, and the dancing lasted all night. We were celebrating victory—victory over so many obstacles that tried to keep them from getting married, but clearly victory over anger and its horrible effects.

The wife had been the subject of a young pregnancy and a physically abusive relationship with the father of her baby. She was able to get out of the relationship and give her life to Jesus. Over the years as a single mother, she grew in health, in spiritual authority, and in freedom from the pain of her past. She forgave this abusive man and let go of her anger, developing a strong but soft heart toward the people around her.

She eventually met a Christian man, who had his own journey of overcoming lust and a painful past. Yet there they were, after years of a faithful dating relationship, with her son as the ring bearer, married under the love and power of Jesus. Their relationship was not characterized by anger and emotional roller coasters. It was characterized by joy, patience, good communication, and a deep love for each other that was rooted in their common commitment to Jesus. Spiritually, the light was shining brightly on this night in a dark city.

In fifteen years of pastoral counseling, I have never met a person who did not struggle with anger. People fall in different places on the type of anger they struggle with, be it passive anger and dealing with the internal fire, or more explosive anger that doesn't have many filters. Regardless of the type of personality, anger is a mighty giant that seeks to keep us from the life that Jesus offers. Anger—or more accurately, how we react to anger—is a clear reminder of the sin cancer that seeks to destroy our lives.

It is telling that, after His introductory comments, the first practical issues Jesus addresses in the Great Sermon are the two giants of anger and sexual impurity. He challenges our understanding on these sins by suggesting that the real problem runs much deeper: anger and lust are just as evil as murder and adultery! Giving in to either leads us towards the fire of hell. Our eternal lives hinge on our honestly seeking to obey Jesus' teaching and conquer our sin cancer at its root, just as we seek to have a truly rooted love of God that empowers us to conquer any worldly love of money.

WHAT GOD SAYS

JESUS GIVES SOME strong commands to us regarding anger in His Great Sermon. Here, in our focus text, He says that if we are angry with someone, we are setting ourselves up to be judged (Matthew 5:22)! It is a strong statement, but Jesus is pushing hard against the influence of the streets that encourage and justify anger.

If we consider all that we have seen so far in the Great Sermon, it is easy to see that Jesus is focused on transforming us into very different people than what the streets produce. The streets are about protecting us from other people, and giving us permission to do whatever it takes to win in the competitions of life. If someone disrespects us, if someone gossips about us, if someone gets in our way, or makes things more difficult, then we are told to feel justified in acting out in our anger. In short, we grow up being taught the rules of anger, what justifies us venting our anger and acting on it. We learn quickly the many different scenarios where we are permitted to act in ways that will bring division to relationships. Simply look at the most popular action movies, and it is clear that revenge is often portrayed as a virtue.

We are often told that getting revenge displays our strength. Jesus is clear that He doesn't flow with that kind of life. Jesus is clear that He is developing very different kinds of people, people who do whatever they can to preserve relationships and minimize the effects of anger. At the beginning of His sermon, when He is dishing out blessings, he doesn't give blessings to those "strong" people who fight for their rights or who have the "strength" to explode on anyone who gets in their way.

In Jesus' world, blessings are given to those who choose humility, mercy, meekness, and making peace between conflicting people (Matthew 5:5-9). Even if people are trying to get us angry, we are still commanded to forgive and push for love and peace (Matthew 5:38-48). Even if there are things in people's lives that are genuinely messed up, we are still not given permission to be angry. We are commanded to focus on our weaknesses, and choose humility (Matthew 7:1-5).

We love to make our gossip session centered on why we should feel good about being angry at someone. Yet Jesus here checks us. He says that if we do not check our anger, if we let it flow freely, He will check us. We are blessed if we choose peace, we are judged if we choose anger. Jesus is bringing some real truth, and it is truth that we desperately need to live more joyful lives. It is not that we are expected to never feel the feeling of anger again. It is that as we let the Spirit of Jesus lead our spirits, when the feeling of anger arises, we work through it in healthy ways that minimizes it and eliminates it, so that our souls can live in joy and peace. Where the streets would encourage us to pour gasoline on the small fire,

Jesus is helping us bring Him into it, so He can put it out completely.

Why is Jesus so tough on anger? Why is He so clear on our need to fight against anger? Because He loves us, and He knows how destructive anger can be to our lives. Anger robs us of joy unlike any other emotion. Anger keeps us from sleeping, keeps us from being able to focus on the good things that are right in front of our faces. Anger twists our thinking and puts irrational thoughts in our heads. All of us can probably think of multiple times in our lives when out of anger we made choices that simply made our lives worse, choices we regretted later.

One of the most extreme examples of the power of anger was hearing about a man in my community who was killed by his friend. It started with an argument over who was going to eat the last piece of pizza. Weeks later it ended in a murder. While most of us probably don't have a story that is so extreme, we can let the extreme stories remind us of how dangerous and destructive it is to simply let anger flow.

LIFE IN THE CITY

JORGE GREW UP in an angry family. His father was a tough man, who earned his living with his hands. Unfortunately, he would often put those same hands on his wife and kids when he got home. Jorge grew up learning to fight and taking his anger out on people in the streets and in bars. Those closest to him nicknamed him "The Hulk" as everyone knew not to make him angry.

Jorge gave his life to Jesus four years ago, and he will be the first to tell you that he went from a man controlled by anger to a man controlled by the love of Jesus. He has story after story that ends with him in shock at the new way he reacted. A year ago, when he and his wife where unemployed and struggling financially, he came out of our church and realized that someone had stolen his truck. Normally he would have reached out to his contacts and found the thieves to not only get his truck back, but to get revenge. Yet, his first reaction was to stop and pray for those who stole the truck, declaring forgiveness over them and asking God to bless them. Later that day it hit him: he was shocked that his first reaction was to forgive. It led him into a deeper awe at God's work of transformation in his heart.

Jorge knows that bringing his anger to Jesus will be a lifelong journey, but everyone who knows him best will tell you that he is a completely different man. I asked Jorge what were the practical things that helped him in his transformation. He said that it was reading the Bible and doing what it said, and building new friendships with Christian men. As he watched their lives, he realized that there was a new way to live, a new way to deal with hurt and anger. He began asking for prayer when he was angry instead of just acting on it.

I wasn't surprised at his response. Obeying the teachings of the Bible and investing in Christian friendships is the meat and potatoes of the new life in Jesus. Being Jorge's friend shows me that there is no excuse. We can't say that our problem with anger is too big to overcome. Time and time again, Jesus has proved through so many of my friends that as we persevere in bringing the instincts of our flesh to Jesus, He will free us from their control over us. He always wins.

GOING FORWARD

ANGER IS ONE of the most destructive emotions we have. Anger is an emotion that regularly and continually challenges us. We cannot conquer it once and be done. Jesus calls us to persistent spiritual discipline, regularly addressing and conquering anger. As frustrating as this unending fight may be, we must remember that our Heavenly Father loves us and is committed to living the journey with us.

Anger is a giant, but it can be overcome. Here are some practical suggestions that have helped me through these struggles.

Anger is not to be trusted

THE STREETS TEACH us to let our anger out immediately. If we are feeling it, then express it. This is bad advice. The main source of anger is feeling hurt by someone or something. When we are hurt and angry, we become irrational and defensive. We see everyone around us through the lens of our emotions—a twisted reality that justifies our anger instead of helping us work through the problem.

Bring your anger to God

INSTEAD OF EXPRESSING your anger in the moment, check it. Bring it to God first, process it with Him, and let Him help you find the root cause. What was it that made you angry? Why? What can you do to deal with the situation in a way that is honest but also honors the heart of God? One of the most important and healthiest habits to develop is going to God first to process our anger instead of blowing up, or trying to bury the anger and move on.

Each case of anger is unique

THERE IS NOT ONE consistent way to handle anger. Sometimes anger is a rational response to a person or situation, and sometimes we allow our twisted perception of reality to build our anger to an exaggerated extreme. Often it helps to process the problem with a trusted and mature friend. In these times of processing, we must be focused on seeing reality rather than having a gossip session. Jesus won't disregard your hurt, but He will lead you to reconciliation and forgiveness.

The Scripture does give us a picture of righteous anger. We see it most clearly in Jesus' reaction to the corruption and abuse in the Temple (Mark 11:15-17). His anger is fueled by the dishonor of God, perpetuation of racial division, and exploitation of the poor. These are some of the issues that should lead us to righteous anger. However, even as we encourage righteous anger, we still need to help each other know how to react to it in ways that will bring God-honoring change to the evils in society.

We are to be very cautious in labeling ourselves as judges over humanity. Only God in his perfection can be trusted to judge those in evil.[35] Righteous anger toward evil should be part of the fuel that keeps us working for holiness and justice, but always with a humility to heed

James 1:19-20, which says, "My dear brothers and sisters, take note of this: Everyone should be quick to listen, slow to speak, and slow to become angry, because human anger does not produce the righteousness that God desires."

You are not a slave to your anger

JESUS PROVIDES everything you need to move past anger and into forgiveness, peace, and joy. It often comes down to a choice between whether we want to be angry people or not. In the end, we are the only ones to blame if we have lived life angry. With Jesus' help, we can stop blaming bosses, co-workers, and family members for our anger. With Jesus, we can stop being a slave to others. If we choose to bring our anger to Jesus, no matter what others do or do not do, He will move us into healing and joy.

We need God in our anger

IN THE FIGHT to conquer anger, we are not going to be perfect. At times we are going to fail and let anger control us. When we do, it is helpful to take time to analyze why we failed. After a blow-up or miscommunication, don't try to move on and forget your failure. Realize that you are a broken person and that Jesus loves you anyway, and then take time to figure out what is at the root of the problem. What triggered this outburst? What lies did you believe? Where were you stubborn? What is causing that stubbornness? How could you have dealt with this in a healthier, God-honoring way? What practical help can you get from a friend to break a bad habit? What are proactive steps you can take before anger consumes you? How can you receive more of Jesus' love to fill up and heal your damaged soul?

A word to parents about anger

RAISING CHILDREN produces a lot of anger. In fact, my kids have caused me more anger than anyone else in my life! (Though the same is true in reverse—they have caused more joy than anyone else as well.) Our most intense emotions with our kids shouldn't always be negative.

A helpful discipline is to choose to be intensely joyful when your kids do something great. When they make right choices or show great attitude, have some crazy fun. Pick them up, yell affirmations at them, pump your fists in the air, create some spontaneous wrestling sessions, and declare to them, "You just made this day amazing!" If they see more intense positive emotions than negative ones, then they will become secure.

When you are angry with your children, question the root. Are you angry for good reason? Did your children exhibit behavior that requires discipline? Or is your anger unjust? Are you allowing your own short temper to influence how you behave towards your kids? It is easy to forget that our kids are struggling against their own sin cancer, and we end up expecting them to be saints. We lose our patience and treat them in ways that we would never want to be treated when we screw up. Discipline is necessary in bringing up children who honor and obey the Lord, but anger is different from healthy, patient discipline. Be careful not to confuse the two.

QUESTIONS TO CONSIDER

1. Why is anger so difficult to deal with?

2. Describe a time you felt victorious over a bad temper, irrational anger, or wanting to use hurtful words.

3. What is your personal action plan for slaying this giant?

---

[35] See Romans 12:14-21.

[36] Ephesians 6:1-4 offers helpful instruction. It shows how both children and parents are to interact in the child-raising process.

CHAPTER TWELVE

SLAYING THE GIANTS, PART THREE
OVERCOMING SEXUAL ADDICTION

*"You have heard that it was said, 'You shall not commit
adultery.' But I tell you that anyone who looks at a woman
lustfully has already committed adultery with her in his
heart. If your right eye causes you to stumble, gouge it
out and throw it away. It is better for you to lose one part
of your body than for your whole body to be thrown into
hell. And if your right hand causes you to stumble, cut it
off and throw it away. It is better for you to lose one part
of your body than for your whole body to go into hell."*

- Matthew 5:27-30

IT IS NOT DIFFICULT to convince people today that sexual
lust is a major issue in our culture. The porn industry
now makes more money annually than the NFL, NBA,
and MLB combined.[37] The issue is convincing people that
dealing with sexual lust is not a casual affair. Recently I
was sitting at a local high school football game and heard
some parents talking about sex among young people. They
kept agreeing that everyone has sex and it is just a part of
growing up. "Nobody gets married a virgin anymore," was
uttered in laughter. It seems like in public conversations,

everyone is very casual and dismissive of sexual lust. Yet, as a pastor who regularly hears people's confessions in private, there is no other issue that even comes close to messing people up.

WHAT GOD SAYS

JUST LIKE ANGER, and the love of money, sexual lust will likely be a never-ending fight. Sexual lust is the desire for the sexually forbidden. Jesus says that anything from lustful thoughts to sexual intercourse outside of marriage is considered adultery. By holding up this spectrum, He is affirming the Old Testament view that sex is only to be experienced within the covenant of marriage. Obviously this is very difficult to live out. Our sin cancer tries to convince us that we actually *need* what we can't have. Whether it's pornography, sexual stimulation, or another person, we need to realize that these desires are misplaced, and we need to continually fight against giving in to them.

1 Corinthians 6:18-20 says, "Flee from sexual immorality. Every other sin a person commits is outside the body, but the sexually immoral person sins against his own body. Do you not know that your bodies are temples of the Holy Spirit, who is in you, whom you have received from God? You are not your own; you were bought at a price. Therefore, honor God with your bodies."

Here we see the same intensity in Paul's teaching ("Flee!") as we do in Jesus' teaching ("Cut it off!"). Why is giving in to sexual desires outside of marriage so spiritually dangerous? Because sex is much more than a physical act. Sex, created by God, is an act of physical, emotional, and spiritual intimacy. We learn elsewhere in Scripture that sex is part of making two people one.[38] The Creator of sex puts a much higher value on sex than the world around us.

Our larger American society views sex as a commodity to pursue. In our consumeristic culture, what we desire we feel entitled to. In fact, the street definition of freedom is the ability to obtain whatever I desire. Tragically, sex has been reduced to simply physical pleasure, something that I should freely pursue for my happiness.

This worldview stands in stark contrast to the teaching of Jesus that we should drastically control our sexual desires and only allow them to be expressed within a lifelong, spiritual, and emotional covenant of marriage. Sexual impurity—including lust—does not only break trust in relationships; it harms your own body. Your body is a temple of God, and He calls us to unite sexually with only one person.

As Paul clarifies in 1 Corinthians 6:19, the Spirit of God dwells within us, giving us the greatest possible intimacy with Jesus. If we let our sexual desires run rampant, we are ruining our ability to live with God's Spirit. We are damaging our intimacy with Jesus, and by default with each other. Those who are the most promiscuous are the least able to have deep, meaningful, consistent, vulnerable relationships. Again, Jesus says that lust is the same as committing adultery (Matthew 5:27). The first step is to rid ourselves of numbness and excuses. We need to see the destructive nature of sexual sin and aggressively flee from it.

LIFE IN THE CITY

WE HAVE A LOT of meetings every week at our church building. Teens and middle school students meet on Wednesday night for pizza, games, and Bible study. Spanish speakers, women's groups, men's groups, co-ed groups, staff meetings, training seminars—there is a lot that goes on in our simple space. However, one of the most inspirational meetings happens every Friday morning at 7:30am before work.

In a small office, a few guys gather to work through a Christian version of the principles of Sexaholics Anonymous. They are diverse in race, class, and life stage, but they are united in their fight for transformation. They meditate on God's truth, they confess their failures to each other, they pray for each other, and they help each other agree to practical changes to gain control over their sexual desires. One man has deleted all the apps on his phone that give him any kind of back door to an Internet browser. One man is going through a ninety-day boot camp of meetings every day to deepen healthy habits and strengthen self-control. One man has been sober for a few years but refuses to slip into a dangerous apathy.

Week after week, they meet up in a small office to leave all their differences at the door. In their humility, we see that the most effective way to build unity is to meet together at the cross, sharing in honest confession and crying out for transformation. They inspire me because they refuse to give up the fight. They help each other stand up to a great ugly giant, with the daily practice of faith that Jesus is greater.

GOING FORWARD

SEXUAL ADDICTION is as entrenched in a person's brain as a drug addiction, thus we need oceans of grace.[39] Sexual sin is one of the strongest manifestations of sin cancer. Unless it is actively dealt with, it grows. Many people's lives are destroyed because they believe the lie that it is good to pursue their sexual desires, a pursuit that tragically leads to addiction. Practically, it is very important to identify the triggers (a certain time of day, a certain emotion, a certain section of town) that lead us to act out. Once we have identified the triggers, we can aggressively put things in place that will help us choose healthy responses to these triggers. Thankfully, Jesus has the love and power we need to overcome this temptation.

It may take time

WE ARE GOING to stumble and fall in this area. Pornography and sex are powerful desires. It often takes years for someone to shake off this addiction, and we need communities of people who are willing to walk alongside each other in this journey—never judging, never condemning, but always holding out love and hope.

Consider how to satisfy the need for true intimacy

SEXUAL LUST, at its root, is actually a desire for intimacy. Sexual addiction can get to the point where it seems like an exclusive physical addiction, but our physical bodies are not separated from our hearts and souls. Think about how our physical stomachs churn when we feel fear or anxiety. In the same way, physical sexual desires are symptoms of a deeper desire to be loved within a deep relationship, without secrets, insecurities, or competition. Jesus offers this. The best proactive step we can take to fight sexual addiction is to deepen our real, raw, dependent, and regular relationship with Jesus.

In fact, one of the great myths within Christian community is that marriage is an ultimate satisfier, as finally we are in a relationship where we can express our sexual desires. While marriage is a gift from God on many levels, marriage does not even come close to providing the solution for sexual addiction and self-control. We do not find our ultimate satisfaction and salvation in marriage intimacy; we find it in intimacy with Jesus.

Rosaria Butterfield captures the intensity of Jesus' teaching on lust with the promise of satisfying intimacy with Him: "What good Christians don't realize is that sexual sin is not recreational sin gone overboard. Sexual sin is predatory. It won't be 'healed' by redeeming the context or the genders. Sexual sin must simply be killed. What is left of your sexuality after this annihilation is up to God. But healing, to the sexual sinner, is death: nothing more and nothing less. I told my audience that I think that too many young Christian fornicators plan that marriage will redeem their sin. Too many young Christian masturbators plan that marriage will redeem their patterns. Too many young Christian Internet pornographers think that having legitimate sex will take away the desire to have illicit sex. They're wrong. And the marriages that result from this line of thinking are dangerous places. I know, I told my audience, why over 50% of Christian marriages end in divorce: because Christians act as though marriage redeems sin. Marriage does not redeem sin. Only Jesus himself can do that."[40]

Hear the truth

WE NEED MORE grace. But we also need more truth! Jesus expects us to conquer lustful thoughts, and to never satisfy sexual desires with anything that is forbidden. I have walked with hundreds of people in this journey. In the early stages, it is easy to believe that we can never be free of pornography and sex. (I know that I believed this in the early stages of my journey.) Then comes the critical fight. After weeks, months, or even years of failure, it is easy to start justifying the gratification: "I am not hurting anyone. This isn't a big deal!" It doesn't help to hear others encouraging us to feed our desires.

There is hope

LET ME SAY that *it is possible* to live a life free from pornography and sex. *It is possible* to be a person who knows how to deal with sexual desires in ways that honor Jesus. It took me years to win this battle, but now I have lived more years as a free man! Though the fight and temptation are never over—I fight just like anyone else—it no longer masters me. The desire to honor Jesus, to honor my wife, my kids, and my church, are stronger than desires of lust. Hope grows as I attack shame with the truth that I am God's kid. I am in the family, and the blood of Jesus flows through my veins.

I often see people start the purity battle strong, but then fall after a month of sobriety. Instead of confessing immediately and getting right back on their feet, instead of remembering that one fall doesn't define their identity, they believe the lies that the one fall means that they are simply addicts, and they start binging for weeks before finally confessing and trying to battle back. When we fall into sin, it is right to own up to the reality that we made a mistake.

It is wrong to believe that we are a mistake. It is wrong to believe that we are just addicts. God's kids get knocked down, but they never get knocked out. They never tap out. When we fall, we get back up, confess our sin, and receive Jesus' declaration of His love for us. Then we just start over with day 1 of sobriety and go longer than we have ever gone before.

"Small" sins lead to "big" ones

MAKING EXCUSES and justifications to watch pornography or regularly pursue personal sexual stimulation only increases an appetite for more. People who cheat on their spouses don't just wake up one day and randomly have sex with another person. Let's not be foolish. It is the habit of giving in to our flesh that eventually makes us want more, and weakens our ability control sexual desire.

Imagine a fireman who sits around all day and never works out, but who keeps telling himself that he will be strong enough when the fires come. Well, months later when he has to carry an unconscious person down six flights in a smoke-filled oven, he will fail. He will collapse, and both will perish! When someone stops justifying the "little pleasures" and starts fighting any and all temptations, they begin to build up "spiritual muscles" that will eventually be ready to resist big temptations. As soon as we stop making excuses and start fighting, Jesus floods into our hearts and takes away the taste for the forbidden. I've seen it so many times!

Try fasting from food

I HAVE FOUND that fasting from food is one of the greatest tools in conquering our addictions to the flesh.[41] As we fast from food, we cause our flesh to suffer and scream for satisfaction. In these moments, we can practice turning to Jesus for satisfaction, which will develop a habit of turning to Jesus when our flesh desires sexual satisfaction. Fasting is such a great spiritual exercise to build spiritual muscles that we will talk more about it in the next chapter.

Confess

CONFESSION IS another powerful tool in winning the fight against sexual addiction and anger. Remember, everything is better in community! Hebrews 3:12-15 and James 5:16 help us see the need to fight sin in community. Overcoming addictive behaviors and entrenched habits as individuals doesn't happen easily. Take courage and talk to a trusted Christian friend. Be completely honest and try to meet once a week to confess your failures from the previous week.

Confession is the best weapon to fight shame. If we let shame fester in our minds and hearts, then we believe the lies that our identity is rooted in our sin. We believe lies that we actually can't overcome. Confession confronts shame head on, and then when we hear forgiveness and affirmation from our friend and from Jesus, we start believing what is true. Our identity is no longer rooted in our sexual desires or our sexual failure, it becomes rooted in Jesus' love for us. As we fight sin, as we succeed and fail, we need our Christian brothers and sisters to remind us of Jesus' forgiveness and to pray grace, healing, power, and conviction over us. Put your fight in the hands of another person and be willing to take their fight. Together you both will see victory. Everything is better in community!

Whatever it takes

JESUS TELLS US in Matthew 5:29-30 that it is better to cut off a limb and enter heaven mutilated than to go to hell with all of our limbs. Thankfully, He is not being literal, but He is being intense! He is saying that we are to have a no-excuses, whatever-it-takes policy in dealing with our sin. We need to install filters on our computers, even if that means dealing with constant crashes. We need to strip our phones of any apps that can lead us to the wrong stuff. We need to check in regularly with a trusted friend, even if that is every day. We must turn our intensity towards cutting off whatever is causing us to sin. After almost twenty years of ministry, I can easily say that the vast majority of people I have worked with who fail to break addictive habits simply refuse to do whatever it takes. They prefer their freedom over their health. They put more intensity in their excuses than they do in cutting things off.

Sizing up the Giants

Greed, anger, and sexual lust are three giants that stand opposing us in the path of following Jesus. Thankfully, we follow a God who loves conquering evil giants. He gives us practical tools and great wisdom. And He keeps drawing us back to Him, reminding us that the heart of this fight is spiritual. For as many boundaries and checks we need to put in our lives, we need to put even more energy into pursuing the heart of God. As we pursue Him, He delights in satisfying us in such complete ways that we begin to develop a distaste for sin and a new fire to gain control over our flesh.

QUESTIONS TO CONSIDER

1. Why is lust so difficult to deal with?

2. Describe a time you felt victorious over impure sexual desire.

3. What is your personal action plan for slaying this giant?

---

[37] ABC News, "Porn Profits: Corporate America's Secret," ABC News, January 28, 2015, accessed November 26, 2016, *abcnews.go.com/Primetime/story?id=132001&page=1*.

[38] See Genesis 2:24, 1 Corinthians 6:15-17.

[39] Valerie Voon, et al., "Neural Correlates of Sexual Cue Reactivity in Individuals with and without Compulsive Sexual Behaviours," *PLoS ONE* 9, no. 7 (2014).

[40] Rosaria Champagne Butterfield, *The Secret Thoughts of an Unlikely Convert: An English Professor's Journey into the Christian Faith* (Pittsburgh: Crown & Covenant Publications, 2012), 83.

[41] When I speak of the "flesh," I am referring to our sinful nature, the part of us that we are born with which is in rebellion to God and infects us with spiritual cancer. See Galatians 5:19-26.

CHAPTER THIRTEEN

SUFFERING

"Blessed are those who hunger and thirst for righteousness, for they will be filled."

- Matthew 5:6

"Blessed are those who are persecuted because of righteousness, for theirs is the kingdom of heaven."

- Matthew 5:10

"If your right eye causes you to stumble, gouge it out and throw it away. It is better for you to lose one part of your body than for your whole body to be thrown into hell. And if your right hand causes you to stumble, cut it off and throw it away. It is better for you to lose one part of your body than for your whole body to go into hell."

- Matthew 5:29-30

MY YOUNGER BROTHER John is an awesome man. He has endured a lot of suffering, and yet, as a result of his relationship with Jesus, he remains one of the most joyful people I know.

When he was in college, he played football. Unfortunately, he tore his ACL in one of his games. For his reconstructive surgery, they replaced his torn ACL with one removed from a recently deceased person. After the surgery, the doctor explained to John that his "new" ACL needed a lot of rehab in order to function. It needed to be stretched and strengthened, and the process would be extremely painful. The doctor told John that his willingness to undergo this pain would determine how fast he would recover.

He was living with my wife and me at the time, and I remember coming home from work and seeing him writhing in pain on the couch, a towel in his mouth to muffle the screams and tears rolling down his cheeks. He had to hook his leg into a machine and then press a button that bent his knee repeatedly. Each bend shot pain through his body; he said it felt as though someone were continually stabbing him in the knee. In spite of this modern-day torture, John kept pushing the button. The pain was caused by the process of stretching and conditioning the new tendon in order for it to heal properly and function well. The more pain he was willing to undergo, the quicker he would heal. There was no other way.

Unfortunately, the same is true for our lives. We are so sick with sin, so infested with spiritual cancer, that the only way we can experience healing is by choosing to undergo the purposeful suffering necessary for our spiritual revival and healing.

One example of how suffering can be beneficial to our spiritual lives is the act of ripping the lust and anger out of our hearts. The process of controlling our thoughts and actions can be uncomfortable, even painful at times, but the more we fight against these impulses, the sooner we will be rid of them. The same is true when it comes to forgiving people who hurt and anger us. It can be painful to sacrifice our righteous anger and bitterness in order to forgive, but it is necessary for the health of our souls. The same is also true when we sacrificially serve others: giving our time and resources can be difficult, but Jesus says that we store up treasure in heaven when we love and serve His people. The only way we can be transformed into people after God's own heart is by purposefully undergoing suffering that breaks down the scar tissue from sin and builds spiritual strength.

WHAT GOD SAYS

THERE ARE TWO types of suffering that we need to step into. The first is fasting from food as a means of boosting our spiritual stamina, and the second is purposeful suffering for the sake of transformation.

In Matthew 6:16-18, Jesus tells us to fast, and to do so in secret. Fasting means abstaining from food—or really any practice for that matter—for a period of time, in order to better focus on God and our transformation.

Fasting has become a lost spiritual practice in American culture. We are a food culture. We don't eat just to satisfy the body's requirements for nutrition and energy; we eat for pleasure. Food is used to "medicate" emotional pain, to deal with anxiety, and to find happiness. Even though we are aware of the many people without food and water in this world, we still spend lots of time and energy pursuing food cravings, or even criticizing bad food experiences. Food has become a central source of pleasure in our lives.[42]

Jesus calls us to fast from food every so often as a means of coming back to the One True God. When we reject physical sustenance, we declare that Jesus, and Jesus alone, can fulfill our deepest needs. While this is the core motivation behind fasting, I have found that fasting from food benefits us another way: it helps us see the reality of our hearts. Without the necessary sustenance our bodies need to function well, we quickly see how easy it is to slip into critical thinking, crankiness, and selfishness. Fasting helps us see how fragile we are: we truly are creatures who need food to survive. Fasting helps us remember that we are not able to independently control our lives or even live without the food God has provided.

It also kills the lusts of the flesh. In my journey to gain control over sexual lust and anger, I have yet to find better medicine than fasting from food. When we fast, our energy levels are lowered, and our physical urges aren't as strong. We don't have the energy to be sexually charged or angry, so we don't give in as quickly when those temptations arise. It makes it easier to take those urges to God and ask Him to perform surgery to remove the root sin. Physical weakness can lead us to Jesus in deeper ways and help us trust Him with our burdens.

If you have never purposefully fasted from food, I strongly urge you to obey Jesus in this way. It will deepen your relationship with Him and help you deal with your sin. There are many good resources available to help you do it well.[43]

The second type of suffering to which God calls us is what I call purposeful suffering. Behind God's call upon us to fast is His desire to lead us toward transformation, through which we are able to have a deeper relationship with Him. The command to fast is another part of a dominant theme in the Great Sermon: we can't fully obey Jesus, follow Him, or be transformed, until we are willing to choose into purposeful suffering.

Jesus is trying to change our worldview here. Life is not about escaping all forms of suffering and living in perpetual comfort. Life is a great, exciting adventure, filled with choices to suffer in order to grow and be transformed. Anyone who preaches a Christianity that will remove all suffering is preaching "American religion." Jesus leads us to the cross of suffering, and we go to it for the joy set before us (Hebrews 12:2).

The purposeful suffering of Christianity is not a one-time rite of passage; rather, it is a way of life. Just as we must choose into exercise (which sometimes causes physical suffering) to maintain a healthy physical body, we must choose into suffering (physical or otherwise) to obtain and maintain the best life with Jesus. A regular reflection on our journey with Jesus should be, "What purposeful suffering is Jesus leading me into for greater transformation?"

Throughout my journey, Jesus has led me to abstain from food, TV, video games, and more. He has asked us to give away all of our savings, have people live with us for long periods of time, and spend time on dangerous streets. Even the call to spend each morning with Jesus and learn how to pray has been full of purposeful suffering. When I attempted to start each day with prayer instead of getting straight to work, it was very difficult! I just wanted to get to work and tackle my to-do list. I was too antsy to sit still with God. So I set my watch for twenty minutes at first, and then gradually increased the time. I made myself sit and try to pray until the watch beeped. Some mornings it felt like torture—time seemed to move so slowly—and I had a hard time keeping my mind focused on prayer. Yet choosing into that simple form of purposeful suffering was the only way to deepen my relationship with Jesus. It was the only way to get to a place where I didn't need a timer to connect with God.

The journey of embracing purposeful suffering for the sake of transformation is never easy. We will fail more often than we succeed. We are all weak and fragile people. As we go through this journey, we must keep a balance: have grace and mercy for the times we fail, but never compromise the instructions and leadership of Jesus. We want to avoid guilt and shame, yet we must also avoid making excuses for our sin or lowering the vision of transformation that Jesus holds out for each of us. We can't look to easier standards or justify our unwillingness to do whatever it takes to obey Jesus. Jesus chose the cross, and as a result he now sits as King of all Kings. The only way to gain eternal life is by following Him. He is our standard. He gives us grace, love, and power to follow Him.

LIFE IN THE CITY

MY FRIENDSHIP WITH Steve has taught me a lot about purposeful suffering. Steve (White-American) and his wife Guadalupe (Mexican-American) have been pillars in our church for the cause of racial reconciliation. Their perseverance doesn't allow any of us to give up on the difficult but beautiful work of unity. Their healthy perspective on Jesus-centered suffering has come from the challenges they have faced in their family.

Steve and Guadalupe have adopted three daughters. Their first daughter they brought home days after her birth. At her six-month checkup they found out that she'd had a stroke before she was born. As a result, major parts of her brain had never developed, and they were told that they would be parenting a non-verbal, severely disabled child with cerebral palsy, a seizure disorder, and cortical blindness. Understandably, they were crushed and spent many nights crying out to God for help in their grief. As their daughter grew and her needs became more intense, Steve and Guadalupe realized that they were being asked to choose into suffering on a daily basis. The condition of their daughter has meant more sleepless nights than good ones, regular digestive problems, and multiple hospitalizations from simple colds that quickly develop into pneumonia. There are no quick fixes for parents of special needs children, as suffering for the sake of love is a daily reality.

Years later after settling in to this unique parenting situation, they adopted two sisters, around late elementary age. These amazing girls had been in and out of several foster homes, which had understandably created difficult emotional and attachment issues. Steve and Guadalupe were told that it would take years to work through these issues, and that some may never be fully resolved. They still said yes, and welcomed the girls into their family.

Steve has cried as many times as anyone from our church when the pressure of his home life overtakes him. Many people stereotype him as a put-together, strong man, simply because he is a tall, educated, White football coach. Yet Steve is as human as any of us. He feels the effects of sacrificial love. He feels the pressure of suffering. What makes him unique is not his ability to handle more than other people. What makes him unique is his ability to trust Jesus in the midst of purposeful suffering.

As a football coach, Steve has had both seasons with teams that win a lot of games and seasons with teams that lose a lot of games. Losing seasons are much more difficult for a head football coach. When you win, everyone praises you. When you lose, everyone suddenly believes they are a better coach than you. During these seasons, I always try to call Steve the morning after losses. I pretend like I call to help him out, but secretly I call to feed my soul.

I love listening to his reflections after these tough losses. He is always able to find Jesus in the midst of people's criticisms or players' bad attitudes. This habit has been formed by his years as a father. He reflects deeply on suffering and its necessity for transformation. His perseverance in loving people, whether it is easy for him or not, always inspires me. I see many people look to him for wisdom in the midst of their trials, the wisdom that has only come as a result of purposeful, Jesus-centered suffering. He embodies Mary Ann Radmacher's quote, "Courage doesn't always roar. Sometimes courage is the quiet voice at the end of the day saying I will try again tomorrow."[44]

Carolina is another one of my inspirations. Her life before Jesus was filled with the suffering of this world. When she was very young, her father left her and her mom, plunging them into grinding poverty. At times they were homeless, and at other times they were living in a small room, without a kitchen or bathroom. As a child she experienced a lot of suffering that God has slowly but surely redeemed.

As a young adult, Carolina said yes to Jesus, and He flooded her heart with joy, healing, and an invitation to *purposeful suffering.* Carolina consistently changes her plans and sacrifices personal comfort to love people. You will see her helping people move, staying up late to counsel a teenager who is in pain, and giving what little money she earns to help another family. She is a gifted translator, and often puts in tremendous hours after work to translate sermons into Spanish for our immigrant community. To top it off, she works at a domestic violence live-in shelter, where she works with women who are at a breaking point of pain and hopelessness.

Carolina embraces seasons of fasting and seasons of prayer. She is becoming a mother figure in our church, mentoring numerous young ladies into following Jesus. I don't know of another person in our community who gets more positive comments and affirmations. God is beginning to speak to her in clear and powerful ways. After years of saying yes to Jesus and embracing sacrificial suffering, we are seeing a leader emerge in our community who shows us the heart of God.

GOING FORWARD

AS WE SEEK God's instruction in the practical areas of our lives, we should not be quick to dismiss paths of obedience that bring suffering. Our spiritual communities should work to hold up the idea that it is normal for Jesus to develop our faith and transform our lives through suffering. I am not referring to masochism, or affirming self-sacrifice as an end in itself. I am referring to Christian communities who are suspicious of the normal American habit of seeking comfort first. What kind of purposeful suffering is Jesus leading you into? Because if He is leading you this way, He is truly leading you toward deeper joy and freedom.[45]

Choosing toward God

IS JESUS CALLING you into the suffering of simple disciplines like setting a timer to increase your prayer muscles? Some of us need to impose disciplines on the kind of movies we watch, what time we go to bed, what we read, or how much time we spend on social media. Some of us need to commit to attending church service or Bible study every week no matter what comes up, regardless of whether we are feeling it. Jesus wants our whole hearts. We don't commit to disciplines simply to achieve something or feel good about ourselves; we regularly evaluate our hearts and let Jesus lead us into whatever kind of discipline will help us follow Him and be transformed into His likeness.

Spiritual disciplines

THERE ARE MANY other spiritual disciplines modeled for us in Scripture. Fasting from food is one. Solitude is another. Jesus often left the busyness of the cities and retreated to the mountains to have time alone with God. What could happen to your life if you left the city for one day every month, found a nice park, and did not bring any technology? There are many spiritual disciplines that we can embrace to follow Jesus and be transformed.[46] Spiritual disciplines are weapons to overcome the struggle we feel taking place within our hearts. Through the disciplines, God is able to remove the sin cancer that is often found in the very same space of our heart where God is seeking to make His home.

Love people who are different and difficult

IS JESUS CALLING you to choose into the glorious suffering of loving those who are difficult for you to love, or who are incredibly different from you? Are you to be the one who finally befriends the co-worker whom nobody talks to? Are you to commit to teaching a group of children at your church even though you don't feel that you have those gifts? Are you to persevere in building relationships with people who live on the other side of town? You may not initially feel like doing this, but Jesus will call you to choose into this purposeful suffering for a greater glory and a greater joy of becoming like Him. (See Chapter 6 for more on this!)

CONCLUSION

IN GENERAL, we don't like discipline. We prefer to be free of all rules, constraints, and boundaries. However, we often forget that in our sin-infected state, we set ourselves up for chaos and destruction if we remove discipline. Think again of a cancer patient working with a doctor. What chance does the patient have of healing if they refuse to submit to the painful work of chemo, diet, and exercise? My brother suffered the physical pain of rehabilitation after surgery, and as a result his knee was soon healthy and functional. What part of your life needs rehabilitation? Where do you need to undergo suffering in order to live healthy, whole lives? What's your version of putting a towel in your mouth, placing your leg in a machine, and pushing the button?

QUESTIONS TO CONSIDER

1. Describe a time when suffering led to growth in your life.

2. Where is God calling you to suffer for your own good?

3. Where is God calling you to suffer for the good of others?

---

[42] For more on the power of food in our lives, see Jan Johnson, *When Food Is Your Best Friend & Worst Enemy* (Toronto: Harper Collins Canada, 1993).

[43] See Matthew 4:1-11 for Jesus' model on how to use food fasting as a powerful weapon to fight the devil. John Piper has put together a great theological and inspirational book on fasting: John Piper, Hunger for God: Desiring God through Fasting and Prayer (Wheaton, IL: Crossway Books, 1997). Mark Nysewander has also written a great practical book on fasting: Mark Nysewander, *The Fasting Key: How You Can Unlock Doors to Spiritual Blessing* (Lancaster, UK: Sovereign World Literature, 2002).

[44] Mary Anne Radmacher, "Home Page," accessed November 26, 2016, *www.mary-anneradmacher.net*.

[45] A recent study found that those who submit to disciplines are more joyful people. See W. Hoffman, et al., "Yes, but are they happy? Effects of trait self-control on affective well-being and life satisfaction," *Journal of Personality* 82, no. 4 (August 2014): 265-77.

[46] Richard Foster has written an excellent book on spiritual disciplines: see Richard Foster, *Celebration of Discipline: The Path to Spiritual Growth* (New York: Harper Collins, 2009). Another great mentor on spiritual disciplines is Dallas Willard: see Dallas Willard, *The Spirit of the Disciplines: Understanding How God Changes Lives* (New York: HarperOne, 2009).

CHAPTER FOURTEEN

SEEK FIRST THE KINGDOM OF GOD

"Therefore I tell you, do not worry about your life, what you will eat or drink; or about your body, what you will wear. Is not life more than food, and the body more than clothes? Look at the birds of the air; they do not sow or reap or store away in barns, and yet your heavenly Father feeds them. Are you not much more valuable than they? Can any one of you by worrying add a single hour to your life?"

"And why do you worry about clothes? See how the flowers of the field grow. They do not labor or spin. Yet I tell you that not even Solomon in all his splendor was dressed like one of these. If that is how God clothes the grass of the field, which is here today and tomorrow is thrown into the fire, will he not much more clothe you—you of little faith? So do not worry, saying, 'What shall we eat?' or 'What shall we drink?' or 'What shall we wear?' For the pagans run after all these things, and your heavenly Father knows that you need them. But seek first his kingdom and his righteousness, and all these things will be given to you as well. Therefore, do not worry about tomorrow, for tomorrow will worry about itself. Each day has enough trouble of its own."

- Matthew 6:25-34

ONCE I SPENT a summer in Mexico City. At one point, the local pastor we were serving with decided to send us to the mountains of Chiapas, a state of Mexico that borders Guatemala. He told us that roughly two hundred indigenous people had just moved there and were trying to settle and establish new lives. They were new Christians, and had all grown up in a community where they used to worship a feared, manipulative, and moody god. They had to sacrifice animals to deal with sin and ask for blessing on a regular basis. Once a year, one member of the family had to run through fire to appease their god.

When these two hundred had learned about Jesus and decided to follow Him instead, the rest of the people from their community began to persecute them. They were treated with social isolation, physical violence, and even death. They were forced to flee to this particular mountain and start over completely.

During the eighteen-hour bus ride to reach them, I kept wondering what we would encounter. I imagined a trauma-stricken, anxiety-ridden people. Our team really didn't know what to expect. As we arrived and began to know the people, we were shocked at what we found.

We expected to help these new Christians, to encourage their faith and build their new community. Instead, they built us up in faith. They lived in little square huts made of sticks, sheet metal, or whatever materials they could find. When we arrived they had just found a well of water higher up in the mountain, and were busy working to pipe that water down into their village. Their joy was amazing, their faith contagious. They kept telling us that God had provided this water source, that He had provided the land.

During the time we were with them, they taught me that Jesus' words that we are looking at in this chapter are true. Seek first His kingdom, and He will take care of your basic needs. God provided water for them because He loved them more than the birds that also lived on that mountain. We never experienced fear or anxiety during our stay with them. Rather, we left with an abundance of joy, faith, and zeal to seek the kingdom of God first, no matter the cost.

Anxiety and fear are great enemies to life with God. When we are fearful and anxious, we can't fully trust in God to take care of us.

WHAT GOD SAYS

JESUS USES LOGIC to counter the emotional condition of fear and anxiety.[47] This logic helps us see that getting our minds in a correct place is the first step towards getting our hearts in a correct place. Jesus desires to make us into people who follow what is true, not what we feel. Let's break down the logic that Jesus presents as to why we should never live in anxiety about the essential needs of our lives.

"Is not life more than food, and the body more than clothing?" If we step back, doesn't life have a much greater purpose than serving our most basic needs? We all have dreams; we all understand that there are greater pursuits for our lives: the nurturing and care of a child, the fireside moments between a husband and wife, the deeper conflicts that beg us to find a solution, the desire to mentor and guide a young person, and the deep longing to look

back on our lives and say that we made a difference. We all share a desire to have our lives count for something greater than working for food, clothes, shelter, and personal entertainment. Perspective can be our best medicine. If you are going to be anxious about anything, be anxious about making your life count, not about how much money is in your bank account. God will provide for your needs, both big and small.

"Look at the birds of the air; they do not sow or reap or store away in barns, and yet your heavenly Father feeds them. Are you not of more value than they?" Wow! What an incredible healing truth! Jesus takes us back to creation and reminds us that we are the pinnacle of God's created order. We are His masterpiece. He has a love for us that is infinitely greater than the love He has for animals. And if He ensures that animals will have their basic needs met, then He will definitely make sure you and I do, too. We really are that special to God.

"Can any one of you by worrying add a single hour to your life?" How does worrying about paying your bills get you any closer to actually paying the bills? Anxious thoughts do nothing to help solve the problem; rather, they make us panic, unable to see or hear God trying to lead us in the midst of our problems. Worrying never adds to our lives; it just takes away peace.

"So do not worry, saying, 'What shall we eat?' or 'What shall we wear?' For the pagans run after all these things." Pagans do not follow or honor God—they live for themselves. They have chosen to trust only in themselves. They have chosen to depend only on their own strength. In making these choices, they run after the basic needs of

this world. They run after more money and more financial security. Jesus is telling us that when it comes to the basic needs of life, when it comes to our financial security, when it comes to our future stability, we are to run after Him! As we choose to run after Him, He will help melt anxiety and give us peace in His strength and provision.

Anxiety is a difficult and often lifelong battle. At times, we seem to conquer it and live in great trust of Jesus. Then life throws us a curve ball and we find ourselves once again in a battle. His words in this section can help us at any time we feel anxiety creep in. Following Jesus means that over time we are no longer driven by anxiety and stress over the basic needs of our lives. Following Jesus means a long journey of deepening trust in God for our basic financial security, even in times of suffering.

"And your heavenly Father knows that you need them." God knows we need food, shelter, clothes, and security. He is not upset about our desire to be taken care of in life. He created us to want these things! Did you notice that Jesus chose to say, "heavenly Father?" A good father knows the needs of his kids, and a good father delights in providing for those needs. God knows what you desire, and He wants to take care of you. You and I can actually choose not to worry because we have a loving, heavenly Father.

Jesus doesn't help us escape our stressful reality with a spa treatment. Jesus gives us the rock-solid truth that it is useless to worry. All we can do is seek first the kingdom. To seek first the Kingdom of God in our lives means that we strive to obey the commands of Jesus more than we strive in any other effort. To seek first the Kingdom means to let the Great Sermon and all other Scripture lead your life. We are to work to live in accordance with God's instructions, and trust that He will take care of us: "Seek first his kingdom and his righteousness, and all these things will be given to you as well" (Matthew 6:33).

Verse 33 is one of those fundamental verses that we need to consistently use to evaluate our lives. Either you are putting your best energies and efforts toward pursuing the needs of your life, or you are putting your best energies and efforts toward obeying Jesus. Either you trust in yourself to meet your needs or you trust in Jesus. We can't fall into the temptation to put both first. We can't try to marry obedience to Jesus with striving to get the best in this life. Jesus calls us to put Him first and then trust Him to provide our needs. At the same time, He gives us a challenging command and a wonderful promise. We can choose to obey His instruction.

LIFE IN THE CITY

GROWING UP IN the city, Carlos and Raquel have never had much money. Yet they were survivors, working different jobs to scrape by. They gave their lives to Jesus four years ago, and everything started to change. One of the first things they asked me to do was a wedding ceremony marking their 15 years together. Their original ceremony was not honoring to God, and they were so high they couldn't remember much of it. They wanted to have another ceremony, saying their vows in the presence of Jesus, and celebrating in the right way.

When they started to follow Him, Jesus began proving to them that He was their provider and that they did not need to worry about the necessities of life. At one point, Raquel lost her job, and Carlos, who works as a carpenter, went on disability because of a severe back injury. Soon after, Raquel's car broke down right before Christmas. They barely made it through the holidays on their disability income.

It seemed like everything was falling apart. But then, out of the blue, a friend of Raquel's who hadn't spoken to her in years called her and offered to give her a car that she no longer needed. This incredible gift of generosity broke anxiety in Carlos and Raquel's heart, and faith began to grow. They realized that God was their provider.

They would tell you that up to this point, they had not trusted God with their finances, had not been organized with their budget, and had not given regularly to church or those in need. That was all about to change.

At a church service in early February, we presented the church with an opportunity to rent the entire second floor of the building we were using, as a means of expanding the church into this space. The tenants had just moved out, and it had become available for potential church use. We needed to know if we could afford the rent, so we asked everyone to anonymously pledge a monthly amount so we could make an informed decision regarding this expansion. Raquel prayed and heard a monthly dollar amount. Carlos approached her and told her that he had also prayed and heard a dollar amount. They shared with each other and found that it was the same amount! However, that amount was more than 20% of their monthly income.

After the gift of a car, they trusted God and started giving that amount every month. They had just agreed a month earlier to be senior leaders in our church, as they were convicted that they needed to seek God's Kingdom first in their community. Their leadership commitment came from a desire to obey Jesus, to live out His commandments for our church and community.

In March, Carlos started getting side jobs that didn't harm his back. He earned a little cash here and there. For five months they gave more than 20% of their meager income and they never ran short for their family's needs. As they headed into the sixth month, Raquel finally got an interview for a new job.

After the first round of interviews, she was asked what she expected to earn if she got the job. They called her two days later to offer her the job and $5,000 more annually than what she requested! For someone who had been unemployed in Los Angeles for half a year, to be offered the one and only job she applied for, and to be offered more money for that job than requested is a miracle!

Carlos and Raquel are some of the most generous people I know. They inspire me to keep giving and to let go of anxiety about my family's needs. They show me what it looks like to seek first the Kingdom!

God's calling and provision to be generous is given to everyone, in every socio-economic sphere. My good friend Tammy grew up in a middle-class, Chinese immigrant household. There were expectations that she would be a successful doctor, which influenced her to enter college as a pre-med student. She was accepted into a highly regarded program at USC. If she maintained a 3.3 GPA in undergrad and had a decent MCAT score, she would be automatically accepted into med school. Early in her freshman year, she heard a sermon on this passage which gave her the conviction to pursue the Kingdom of God first as a college student.

A year later, this meant saying yes to a summer program where she would live in an urban poor community of Los Angeles and serve a local church. The summer program and a deeper study of Scripture opened her eyes to the world of the urban poor and to God's heart to walk with the poor.

She finished the summer questioning whether God wanted her to be a doctor, but sure that He wanted her to build deeper relationships with people very different from her. As she voiced her confusion about her future career path to her parents, they were not happy. They increased their pressure on her to become a doctor. She took the MCAT test and did poorly, losing her guarantee to be accepted into medical school. This devastated her parents, but in the painful conversations with them, she heard God say, "If you continue to invest in the poor, your future as a doctor is in my hands."

Instead of using the following summer to claw her way back into med school, she signed up again to live and serve in an urban poor community! She still applied to medical school and shockingly got in without any interviews. It ended up being a "mistake"—they forgot to take her out of the automatic acceptance program after doing poorly on the MCAT! She scheduled a meeting with the dean, who surprisingly said, "Well, let's do an interview and see what happens." In the interview, she realized that the interviewer was totally sympathetic to her as she shared about her convictions and the years she spent investing in her relationship with Jesus and the urban poor! She left the interview unsure of her future in medicine, but more sure of pursuing Jesus and his heart for the poor.

As she entered her final semester as an undergrad, she applied and was accepted into a two-year internship with Servant Partners, a non-profit Christian organization, to live and serve in urban Los Angeles. After being accepted into the internship, she received the official acceptance into medical school! Hold on, it gets even better! She realized that God was totally faithful to His word about backing her up as she continued to pursue His Kingdom first, so she asked the dean if she could defer the acceptance for two years to do the internship among the urban poor. Nobody asks for a two-year deferment to med school. But the dean approved! Seek first the Kingdom of God...and all these things will be given to you as well.

Two years later she started medical school. By her own report, Tammy says that by the time she started her studies there, she was a different woman. It was clear to her that God wanted her to be a doctor, but it also became clear to her that He needed to shape her heart to be like His.

She is currently living in East LA, working as a family physician in one of the best hospitals for the urban poor. She not only gets to work with patients that she lives in the same neighborhood with, she gets to train a new generation of doctors to see the poor with the same heart and dignity of Jesus.

The best part of the story? Her parents, who were even angrier at her two-year deferment, are now completely supportive. They had always been Christian, but through Tammy's determination to trust God's will, they have developed a new heart for the urban poor, and a new definition of success in the Kingdom of God. Every time I talk with Tammy about her incredible life, I am reminded that when we have the courage to practically change our lives to seek first the Kingdom, God will always provide for us, and in much better ways than we could provide for ourselves.

GOING FORWARD

INSTEAD OF SEEKING after the needs of this life, seek after the eternal, both for your own life as well as for all the lives around you. Remember that to seek first the Kingdom of God means to do everything that Jesus talks about in this Great Sermon. It means to put our best energy, time, money, and work ethic into being people who love God more than anything else, who know how to spend time with Him, who relentlessly obey His directives, who love people as eternal treasure, who work to forgive, who love our enemies, and who seek to reconcile conflicts. It means owning up to our sin cancer so we are no longer dominated by anger, lust, anxiety, or greed. It means doing everything we can to live life as an ambassador of Jesus in a world full of chaos. It means being consumed with the eternal things of God and His kids, more than by what food we will eat at the end of the month, whether we can buy that new car, get a job promotion, build our investment portfolios, and pay for college tuitions.

Hear the words of Jesus again: "Seek first his kingdom and his righteousness, and all these things will be given to you." Sadly, the culture and pattern for American Christianity has become, "Seek first your own provision, the stuff, the needs, and the wealth for great security, and *then* fit God into all of that." This behavior has been created by anxious thought patterns. Let's be people of faith who trust in a God who knows our needs, who is able to provide for our every need, and who loves us a hundred times more than the beautiful animals He created and provides for every day.

At the end of this life, I don't think anyone will look back and wish they had acquired more things, or worried more about the basic needs of life. I think people will look back and wish they had spent more time with the people they loved. I think they will look back and wish they had risked more, that they had lived with more courage and love.

I want to have lived the kind of life that causes my children to stand up at my funeral and declare, "There is one thing that our dad showed us, and that was how to seek first the kingdom of God. He was and is the richest person we have ever known."

QUESTIONS TO CONSIDER

1. What things does society tell you to "seek first"?

2. What was a time you caught yourself stressing out about something God promised to take care of? What worries do you need to give to God today?

3. How do you need to seek God's kingdom first in your life?

---

[47] In our world today, the word 'anxiety' sometimes describes a medical issue that can even have physical causes inside a person's brain. I'm instead using the word the way Jesus used it—to describe the common attitude of being worried about the future, like stressing about getting the bills paid and avoiding accidents. Those with the medical condition should talk to both Jesus AND their doctor about how to find healing.

CHAPTER FIFTEEN

WORLD CHANGERS: BEING AN AMBASSADOR OF JESUS TO THE WORLD

"Blessed are the meek, for they will inherit the EARTH."

- Matthew 5:5

"You are the salt of the EARTH."

- Matthew 5:13

"You are the light of the WORLD."

- Matthew 5:14

"This, then, is how you should pray:

'Our father in HEAVEN, hallowed be your name,

*your kingdom come, your will be done
on EARTH as it is in HEAVEN.'"*

- Matthew 6:9-10 (Capitalization added)

I KNOW A WOMAN who followed Jesus to serve in Africa for a summer, living among some of the world's poorest people. As she sat on the long plane ride, she was bursting with excitement, wanting to make a difference for

Jesus in Africa. She wanted to help hundreds of people by showing them a new life that Jesus offers. But when she arrived, her excitement quickly faded away. She had committed to work for a local African church, but after meeting the leadership team, she was told that she would be spending her summer doing housework for a local family. Initially, she chafed at this and wrestled in her spirit: why had she given up her time and money just to cook and clean for a local family? But slowly she found Jesus in her work and gained more joy for the unseen labor of love. She embraced the daily call of servanthood and began to realize that her summer work was indeed a calling from God: living as a servant was transforming her heart. She began to see all the ways Jesus was giving her opportunities to become like Him.

As she was saying goodbye on her last day, the African leadership of the church approached her. They thanked her profusely and told her that she was the first American missionary they had worked with who was willing to serve African leadership. They had almost decided to stop working with American Christians (those who came to preach, but not live out the Great Sermon), but after witnessing her servanthood they were ready to accept any future missionaries from her church.

You can imagine the joy she felt on the plane ride home. She trusted Jesus to live humbly, and by gaining the trust of an African community, she truly "inherited the earth." In her servanthood, she was a light in Africa, exemplifying the love of Jesus and bringing healing, unity, and future partnerships.

WHAT GOD SAYS

IN THE BEGINNING of the Great Sermon, Jesus tells His disciples that they are the light of the world. He then goes on to teach about how to become that light. Consider the kind of people we would be if we trusted Jesus and obeyed all of His instructions in the Great Sermon. We would become people who:

✓ are characterized by a genuine humility and peace

✓ own up to our sin cancer on a regular basis

✓ choose to serve in unseen ways and do the things nobody else wants to do

✓ work to build real relationships with those whom society ignores

✓ work to unify people who have deep differences

✓ do not hold grudges but regularly reconcile

✓ actively work to bless and forgive our enemies

✓ give generously and sacrificially

✓ strive for purity of heart and righteousness

✓ grow in self-control over anger and lust

✓ choose into purposeful suffering for the greater good

✓ are characterized by an enduring peace in the face of all suffering

✓ are free from anxiety and confident in a loving Father who loves to provide the necessities of life

✓ have a real, honest, thriving, and life-centering relationship with Jesus!

This is a description of a person who will challenge people in healthy ways, heal people from great brokenness, offer hope, build trust, and bring leadership! This is the description of a person who exemplifies Jesus for everyone they meet. This is a description of a world changer. This is the description of someone who brings light into darkness.

It is not that we are expected to be perfect. Jesus explains in Matthew 26 that He, and He alone, is the flawless one, offering His blood as a covenant of forgiveness for us.[48] While we are not to be perfect, in light of His constant forgiveness, we are to pursue total obedience to Jesus. Transformation is a lifetime of obedience, not a quick change. If we strive to become this kind of person, we don't need fancy skills, flashy personalities, smooth talking, or complicated strategies. *Our message will be heard because it will be clearly seen.*

It strikes me that before Jesus tells His disciples that they will be the light of the world, He declares that the meek will inherit the earth. He seems to be emphasizing that loud, brash, wealth-driven, power-seeking leadership is not going to capture the hearts of those lost in darkness. The meek inherit the earth; the meek gain authority in the earth. Meekness in this context certainly doesn't imply fear. Jesus makes it clear that the meek are to shine their light into the world.

This kind of authority—set within the meekness of obedience to Jesus—comes because as people who follow

Jesus we choose not to be afraid. We do not hide behind our weaknesses, or our perceived lack of gifts, wealth, and charisma, nor do we put our identity and strength in any gifts, wealth, or charisma we do have. We obey Jesus, He transforms us, and the world sees light! Spiritual authority in this world comes through obedience to Jesus, and not through any other means. We must stop covering our light, and we must start making intentional choices to be servant-leaders, influencers, and ambassadors of the kingdom of God.

LIFE IN THE CITY

MY FRIEND MARIA Hermelinda is a light in this world. She had her son as a teenager, and eventually split from her son's father because of his abuse. Making the transition to being a single mom in her early twenties was not easy, and it left a lot of anger in her heart. Part of her anger was directed at God. For her college English class, she wrote a paper on the foolishness of Christians believing in a loving God. The week she turned the paper in, she was invited to a Bible study by a friend. She went more out of cynicism than curiosity. She didn't expect Jesus to leap out of the pages of the Bible and melt away the anger of her heart.

Some time later, she gave her life to Jesus. Maria has never been the confident leader type, but she has always exhibited a faithful perseverance. She works two jobs to handle the expenses of a now pre-teen and growing boy. She serves in various capacities in our church, and is regularly confessing sin and working on her character and intimacy with Jesus.

Last year, she said yes to go to Malawi, Africa with a team of missionaries to work among Muslim tribes in the south. She said that from the moment she arrived, she felt insecure, as the other members of her team had been following Jesus much longer, had more leadership experience, and just seemed to have more gifts.

As the days passed in these villages, the team was trying to figure out how to navigate the sensitive path of working with Muslims. One day, Maria was sitting in the dirt with a bunch of Muslim women, when all of a sudden the translator asked Maria to talk to them. At first, Maria hesitated, nervous about what to say. The translator encouraged her to simply share her story, so she did.

The more details she shared about the struggles of growing up in our community, the more the women began to engage. As she began to share about having her son and the abuse of his father, the women became very animated. It startled her and she asked the translator what was going on. The translator said that they were all relating to her and agreeing with her. They were asking her to explain to them how she had found happiness after so much pain.

Maria took a deep breath and started sharing about Jesus. When she was done, the translator encouraged her to ask if any of the women there wanted to have a relationship with Jesus. When she asked, all the women said yes. Maria began to pray with them. This one vulnerable conversation forged a whole new openness for the Gospel in their tribe, and the women were left with a new hope.

Maria is not a superhero. At the end of the day, all of her experiences in Malawi and East LA are serving Jesus' ultimate purpose of transforming her heart into His likeness—a calling we all share. But by engaging the world along with Jesus, she is living a life that is about more than just self-satisfaction and self-survival. Instead of wasting her life, consumed with building things that are temporary, she has received the undeserved invitation to build the kingdom of God. Wow!

Maria doesn't have seminary training or extraordinary leadership skills, but ever since the first day she said yes to Jesus, she has been surrendering her life to His leadership. She evaluates her life by the Great Sermon. She makes intentional choices to care for people and speak about Jesus. His light keeps shining brighter and brighter through her. Maria was following Jesus in East LA, but God had something more for her. He wanted her to have a global perspective, and for her this meant travelling to Malawi, Africa. Now, people in her life are starting to realize that Maria has found the treasure of God's presence and power that they have been searching for their entire lives, and they want some of it!

Whether it is personally going to other countries, praying for other countries, giving money to support God's work in other countries, or making some other connection, the Great Sermon emphasizes the fact that those who follow Jesus are given everything they need to change the world. We are given Jesus in order to shine brightly within the world.

GOING FORWARD

WOULDN'T IT BE sad if, at the end of your life, people said you were most passionate when you discovered great food at a new restaurant, or the new TV drama that was so awesome? Wouldn't you feel regret if you were known more for your passion for sports than your love of Jesus and people in need? When people see you striving after the holiness described in the Sermon on the Mount with the same genuine passion you have for fantasy football, finding great shopping deals, keeping up with pop culture, buying new gadgets, or hearing new gossip, then people will want to know more about what you have found in Jesus.

It is important that we seek to overcome any obstacles that keep us from shining our light and becoming the world-changers that God has called and made us to be. There are several things to remember as we do this.

Overcome fear

ONE REASON WE hide our light is fear. Social acceptance is a powerful value in America. Many people passionately pursue fitting in, going with the flow, and not sticking out because the thought of being mocked, laughed at, or disagreed with is a great fear. I too, often feel these social fears. However, *fear is the greatest enemy to faith.*[49]

Knowing where to start

ANOTHER BIG OBSTACLE to becoming a world-changer is not knowing what to do, where to start, or where to go.

There are thousands of needs all around us, and it can feel overwhelming. However, as you become more serious about obeying the commands of Jesus in the Great Sermon, you can expect that people will start to come to you. When people in darkness suddenly see a light, they seek it. So start obeying, and then ask God for eyes to see what He will bring. Practically, commit to the ways your church is striving to be a light in your community and the world. Instead of trying to forge your own independent path, commit to join hands with your spiritual family to shine light. As we talked about in chapter 7, it is simply impossible to be transformed into the likeness of Jesus without a deep commitment to a community of believers.

It's God's work

THE GOAL OF following Jesus is not to invent some great plan to save the world. God has done the work to bring salvation to us—just read one of the Gospels. We don't need to create a new flashy ministry. We just need to take one step at a time. We need to make small choices and begin seeing our communities differently. The more we obey Jesus, the more we'll see people the way He sees them—people to forgive and love. The more our days are centered on Jesus, the less we will worry about our own lives, focusing instead on the needs of others.

Have a global perspective

ESPECIALLY IN URBAN poor communities, it is easy to be consumed with the overwhelming amount of needs within a small area. As churches and individuals, we must regularly take steps to be lights in our immediate area, and regularly offer the love and power of Jesus to our neighbors. Yet we also need to remember that we are ambassadors to the whole world.

Followers of Jesus should be global-minded, dedicated to changing the world. We should start learning about what is happening around the world, pray on a regular basis for countries and people groups who have little or no connection to Jesus, and then go to those nations that God leads our churches to. It sounds simple, but the best way to be a world-changer is to put yourself in places that need to be changed. Seek out God's unique call on your life and be secure to find your place in His mission. Not every sphere or role is for everyone. We are a part of a huge family. Jesus will lead us to the role He created us to achieve. We can be secure knowing that our role is as significant as any other.

Live out the Great Sermon

JESUS' LAST WORDS to the original disciples in the Gospel of Matthew are, "Therefore go and make disciples of all nations, baptizing them in the name of the Father and of the Son and of the Holy Spirit, *and teaching them to obey everything I have commanded you.* And surely I am with you always, to the very end of the age." (Matthew 28:19-20, emphasis mine). When Matthew wrote his gospel, he was not working with a copy of the New Testament. Thus, it is important to ask ourselves, "What are the teachings we are to share? What commands did Jesus give us?" The Gospel of Matthew contains a great deal of Jesus' teachings, through parables and dialogue. However, the core teaching of Jesus in the Gospel of Matthew is found in chapters

5-7, in what I am calling the Great Sermon. In these final words, Jesus is essentially telling His disciples to go live out the Great Sermon and teach others to do the same.

The ultimate goal for us is to become world-changers

AS WE JOURNEY through the Great Sermon, we must stop and realize that every challenge Jesus gives us, every call for change in our lives, every instruction to our heart and for the transformation of our character is ultimately for the purpose of becoming salt to the earth and light to the world. The goal of this life change is to take one who is a slave to sin cancer and mold them to be more like Christ, so that when people see them, the first thing they see is an ambassador of Jesus. Jesus' ultimate hope for your life is not just to make you a better person, though that is part of it, but to make you a world-changer!

You are made to be a light that shines in dark places. You are made to be salt in the earth, to bring the "taste" into whole communities that have gone stale. In the Great Sermon, Jesus tells His disciples to be salt and light, and then He gives us practical instruction on how to do just that. He tells us how to be transformed in our hearts, minds, and character. All Jesus asks of us is to say yes to a daily journey of becoming like Him!

The more our lives resemble Jesus' life, the saltier our salt and the brighter our light! You were called by Jesus to change people's lives for eternity. It is so crucial to realize that, in this Great Sermon, Jesus never talks about strategy; He never talks about having a certain personality, a certain amount of wealth, or certain gifts. He invites us to follow Him, to become like Him. He invites you!

Trust Jesus. Be courageous. Be a light. Take real steps to change the world.

QUESTIONS TO CONSIDER

1. Who do you look to as an example of a world changer?

2. What are some ways you hope the world will be different because of Jesus' presence within you?

3. What do you need to change about your life to be salt and light for the world in this way?

[48] Matthew 26:26-29.

[49] This is a central theme of the gospel of Mark. Consider 4:39-41, 5:14-17, 5:32-34, 5:36, 6:26, 6:49-52, 8:34-38, 9:21-25, 10:22, 10:46-52, 14:50, 14:66-72, 16:8.

CHAPTER SIXTEEN

MAKING DISCIPLES

"Now when Jesus saw the crowds, he went up on a mountainside and sat down. His disciples came to him."

- Matthew 5:1

"Therefore go and make disciples of all nations, baptizing them in the name of the Father and of the Son and of the Holy Spirit and teaching them to obey everything I have commanded you. And surely I am with you always, to the very end of the age."

- Matthew 28:19-20

ONE OF THE MOST significant moments in my life was sitting down as a twenty-year-old with my college pastor, and hearing him say, "I would like to disciple you in the faith. If you are willing, I will commit to a friendship with you and pass onto you all that has been passed onto me. My hope is that for the rest of your life, you disciple as many people as you can."

The Great Sermon is given to Jesus' disciples. It is His blueprint for following Him, thinking like Him, and having His heart. In the end, we can't be like Jesus if we are not committed to making disciples. Jesus is about loving and transforming people. If Jesus lives inside of us, then we too are about loving and transforming people.

As we saw at the very beginning of this study, Jesus makes a big statement about what it means to follow Him. He stops the display of power and gives the Great Sermon to teach about deep, foundational, holistic disciple making. Jesus is not about flashy faith or quick fixes. A friend of mine said, "Modern Christianity prides itself in having a big flashy house built on the sand (great teaching, professional production, powerful music, and influence in numbers), rather than a small house that has been slowly built on a great foundation."

WHAT GOD SAYS

JESUS SPENT MORE time walking with twelve people than He did teaching large crowds. Jesus spent more time encouraging, teaching, and holding accountable twelve people than He did preaching to stadiums. From His model, we can define discipleship as one person helping another person become an obedient follower of Jesus. What does this look like practically?

It means two or three people meeting together on a weekly basis, sometimes more, sharing the good and bad parts of their lives, studying the teachings of Jesus, and then obeying those teachings together. It means these people choose to be in each other's lives, and walk together in becoming like Jesus. Ideally, someone who is further along the journey will help a person just starting out in the journey. In this scenario, there is transparency, accountability, and an effort from the leader to help the younger person into self-discovery. In this relationship, preaching and lecturing are at a minimum, and asking questions with reflection on the Scripture is at the center.

As Jesus did, the leader should model obedience in all areas, and love the person being discipled as Jesus loves them. When a discipleship relationship comes to an end (in the best scenario, when the person being discipled is ready to disciple another), the person who has been discipled should be able to say, "I experienced God's love for me through my friend. That love has changed my life."

Making a commitment to invest in another person's life is not easy. To be able to walk with them as they deal with sin cancer and the struggles of obeying Jesus will prove difficult. Some discipleship meetings are a little slow and mundane, or feel like nothing is changing. There won't be fireworks every time two or three people meet for accountability and help in their spiritual growth. It is so much more exciting to go to a big worship conference or a short-term mission trip than it is to commit to the daily tasks of following Jesus. Yet it is the mundane, consistent choices of investment in another person and obeying the word of God together that really have the power to change the world. Day-to-day relationships that are consistent in the demonstration of both servant love and applying the truth of Scripture to life can bring more transformation than any mountaintop conference experience.

Of course, the power of God will always be in the journey; we will see miracles and we will experience the joy of worshiping with others. But it is only through discipleship together that we will build lives of transformation.

LIFE IN THE CITY

I SHARED A LITTLE about Jorge's journey earlier in this book. Jorge has become an incredible friend as I have discipled him over these past years. Almost two years ago, Jorge believed that he could begin stepping into the call to disciple others. Jorge never finished college, he doesn't have a seminary degree, and he started following Jesus after he was forty. However, he has obeyed Jesus and his life has radically changed. Family members are shocked at the different man that he is, and some are now calling him the family pastor.

One of his brothers-in-law, Paul, was dealing with a serious drug addiction that had him living on and off Skid Row, LA's largest homeless community. Paul also had some problems with Jorge, as they almost got into a fist-fight at a family party before Jorge knew Jesus. Yet, as Paul hung around Jorge and saw the transformation, he began to yearn for the same Jesus that Jorge knew.

Soon Paul said yes to following Jesus, and then also to being part of a discipleship time with Jorge. Jorge now brings Paul to his small side jobs and trains Paul in carpentry and other construction skills. On the drive to and from work and during their lunch break, Jorge teaches Paul the Bible, and helps him think through how to bring Jesus into every part of his life. Many times, the two of them will also pull another co-worker into the conversation, and share the Gospel.

Jorge and Paul have now become great friends, and Paul's life is changing. Last Easter, in front of our church and Paul's family, Jorge baptized Paul. That service is still the largest service we have ever had in the history of our little church.

Paul's parents were Christians and had been praying for him for decades. Just a few months after Paul's baptism, Paul's father died. Yet he died in great joy, knowing that his son was now following Jesus. Paul continues to grow and give testimonies of God's work in his life. Jorge will always be great friends with Paul, and he continues to support him in his journey. Jorge has now seen the transformative power of discipleship, and he's getting ready to invest in another disciple new to the faith. He has decided that from this point forward, he will lay down his life in love, to help as many people as possible grow in the love of Jesus.

In the end, that is what life with Jesus is all about. Jesus overwhelms us with His love. He defeats our sin through love. He changes the world through love. When He calls us to make disciples, He is giving us another prescription for our own transformation: share My love with My people. We need His love to overcome our fears, insecurities, and comforts, and to step into another person's life.[50]

GOING FORWARD

IN MOVING TOWARD discipleship relationships, we often meet certain obstacles that need to be overcome. A few of these obstacles are given here.

A desire to be "perfect" before we begin

WE ARE NOT obeying Jesus in our own lives, so we don't feel like we can encourage others to obey.

WHAT TO DO: Our failures do not disqualify us from discipling others. If we choose to share our failures with the person we are discipling, and even better, if we choose to model healthy repentance when we fail, we are more than qualified to disciple! It is very difficult for someone who is young in faith to be discipled by a "perfect person." We need to model the incredible love of our Father in heaven by confessing our mistakes and owning up to our sin cancer, and then receiving the kind of love that fuels a new conviction to live differently. But if we choose to live in darkness and ignore our sin cancer, then we should not disciple anyone.

Busy schedules

OFTEN, WE DON'T want to sacrifice the time and energy it takes to intentionally commit to someone else's growth. It is much more comfortable to go to church meetings than it is to roll up our sleeves and sacrificially love someone as a brother or sister in Jesus.

WHAT TO DO: We have to help each other step back and reflect on what is non-negotiable in our lives: God and other people. We have to remember what gives us the best joy. At the end of our lives, will we want to look back and see that we went to a lot of events, kept up with the trending television shows, and pursued lots of hobbies? Or will we want to look back and see that we discipled twenty people into Jesus-centered transformation, who are now discipling other people, who are discipling even more people? There is always time to commit to another person if that is a priority in our lives. We all have the same amount of time. Life with Jesus is about using that time to be His disciple and helping other people be His disciples.

Fear of failure

WE ARE OFTEN afraid that the person we walk with won't change, or will feel disappointed in us for failing them in some way.

WHAT TO DO: Jesus' call to make disciples is given alongside His power and presence. He tells us that He has all the authority, and that He will always be with us. We can't transform anybody! Only Jesus transforms. We can't put our identity and self-worth into the results of our discipleship relationships. Discipleship is not about us; it is about Jesus. I have had many discipleship relationships end poorly for various reasons. Sometimes the person doesn't want to grow and gets stuck in some area of stubbornness. Sometimes I don't exercise enough wisdom and I rush into a discipleship relationship before that person is ready for transformation. Sometimes relationships just don't gel. But in the end I could move on because I knew that my actions came from love.

A lack of practical steps and tools

OFTEN PEOPLE ASK me if I use a curriculum or book to help me disciple others in following Jesus. I have used several, and I hope that this book will prove useful to you as well. Regardless of the text used, the discipleship immersion should roughly follow a standard arc.

WHAT TO DO: First, it depends on where the person is in their faith journey. If we start discipling someone brand new to the faith, we want to give them a good foundation of life as a Jesus follower and a basic understanding of the discipleship journey, which can be summarized by being transformed in our three core relationships: relationship with God, relationship with the church, and relationship with the world.

It is important to make sure they understand their relationship to God. Their identity is now in Jesus; they have been saved by God. They are not able to save themselves and are empowered to transform through the grace and power of God, not by their own efforts apart from God. It is crucial that they understand their new identity and the ongoing work of grace and God's power in their life so that they embrace all of His commands with faith that He will give them the power to obey.

Then, in any discipling relationship, we want to figure out where God is working in their lives. Where is God pressing them to trust Him, to grow in faith, or to fight a particular sin? We want to partner with God in the transformational process instead of blindly bringing in some curriculum or outside agenda. As we ask questions, listen to their story and their heart, we can then encourage them to greater obedience in the issues that God is already stirring up in them.

Once we've settled into a consistent pattern of walking together, then we can use the Great Sermon as a starting place. Take one passage at a time, talk through it, share vulnerably about how the passage has challenged your life, and then brainstorm together how you both can obey the teaching. Use the Discipling Plan in Appendix A as an aid to help you in the journey.

When reading the Sermon on the Mount, ask God to give you other Scriptures to reflect on together and obey. The litmus test of a good discipling relationship is that the person is developing a deeper, more consistent heart of hearing God speak and obeying what is heard. If you help someone make that the central part of their life, it is time to celebrate!

Remember, Jesus started His ministry by defeating the devil in the wilderness, followed by three verses of power ministry where the sick are healed and demons are cast out.[51] An objective reader would think that a large-scale revival all about healing and deliverance is about to break out. But just as that seems to start, Jesus walks up to a mountain, with His disciples, and He teaches them three chapters of the counterintuitive but transformative daily path of being His disciples.

Making disciples does include leading people into the power of God, moments of healing, hearing the voice of God, and defeating demons. However, the engine that advances the Kingdom of God on this earth is discipleship. It is individuals and churches obeying the teachings of Jesus and helping others do the same.

To that end, Jesus came to start a discipleship revolution, one that would create communities of disciples in every city all over the world. These communities of disciples are to be lights to their cities, showing everyone an alternative way of dealing with power, differences, money, marriage and more. It is not about finding a new way to change the world; it is about embracing the way of Jesus, and obeying Him with every part of our lives. Be a disciple. Make disciples. Watch the transformation begin!

QUESTIONS TO CONSIDER

1. Have you ever been discipled, or mentored, by another Christian? If so, share about it.

2. Do you need to be discipled now, or are you ready to disciple others?

3. Whom might God be calling you to disciple?

---

[50] For a great book on the "how to's" of discipling others, see Robert Herber, *Changing the World through Discipleship* (San Diego: All People's Church, 2011).

[51] Matthew 4:23-25.

CHAPTER SEVENTEEN

THE JOURNEY OF TODAY: LIVING IN THE PRESENT

"Give us today our daily bread."

- Matthew 6:11

"But seek first his kingdom and his righteousness, and all these things will be given to you as well. Therefore, do not worry about tomorrow, for tomorrow will worry about itself. Each day has enough trouble of its own."

- Matthew 6:33-34

SEVERAL YEARS AGO, a good friend of mine realized that he was addicted to bad food. He was tired of what it was doing to his weight and health. After some community processing, he decided to commit to an Overeaters Anonymous program (OA). During the year he was in the program, his life changed drastically. He lost weight, gained greater self-control, and started living with a deeper reserve of joy. I learned so much by watching and listening to my friend as he walked through the program.

There are two pillars that anchor OA. The first is to own up to your problem and your need for help, with no excuses. My friend experienced freedom from his guilt and shame, simply by admitting his problem in a community and receiving their unconditional love and forgiveness. This experience taught me the great power of humility and exemplified the great healing power that comes with the love and forgiveness of Jesus. Just as my friend did in his program, we too can stand in the love of our heavenly Father, face our sin, and conquer it.

The other pillar of OA is the commitment to simply "live for today." There are no long-range goals, no thirty or sixty-day crash diets, just individuals creating an eating lifestyle that works on a daily basis. My friend decided that he wanted to exercise every day and that he did not want to snack between meals, eat fast food, or have more than one full plate of food at meals. Once he decided how he wanted to live during a normal day, he was only responsible for being faithful to his goals today. If he screwed up, he talked about it with a mentor from the program and then woke up the next day, ready to do his best to live for that day.

As I walked with my friend through that year, it was obvious to me that God was using his journey to bring me back to a fundamental pillar of Christianity: live to be faithful today.

We have strayed a long way from this pillar. Because church meetings are once a week, sometimes twice, we have unconsciously made our practical faith a weekly routine, relying on this one meeting to somehow sustain us throughout the rest of the week. We are like a hamster running in its wheel, giving some effort, but never seeing any transformation. Instead, we need to come to God daily, and seek from Him our daily bread. Because of the immensity of our sin cancer, we cannot hope to live out the Great Sermon on our own for even one day! We need the daily help of Jesus to live in faith, courage, generosity, sacrificial love, forgiveness, and self-control. Until this sinks in, we will continue to run in circles, with sporadic efforts at change, always ending in the same place. This is what I learned about myself as I watched my friend receive daily help from his OA community.

WHAT GOD SAYS

WHEN JESUS TEACHES us how to pray the Lord's Prayer (Matthew 6:9-13), the expectation is that we will pray daily: "Give us today our daily bread." This expectation, coupled with the content of the prayer, implies that we are also to ask for forgiveness today, to forgive today, to honor and worship His name and character today, to pray for His kingdom to grow today, and to ask for help with temptation today.

Matthew 6:34 says, "Therefore do not worry about tomorrow, for tomorrow will worry about itself. Each day has enough trouble of its own." The focus, again, is on living for today. Today you have people who will stir up fresh anger. Today you have children who will need to be loved. Today you have temptations to fight. Today you have fears and doubts to battle. Today you have to fight for joy. Today you have opportunities to act courageously, to speak about the greatness of Jesus, to be a peacemaker, to be sacrificial with your money, and to comfort someone in need. Tomorrow will take care of its own worries (Matthew 6:34). Strive to serve Jesus today! Fight to follow His lead today.

LIFE IN THE CITY

LORETTA IS A FRIEND who understands what it means to with Jesus today. She has had a life of chaos, growing up in grinding poverty in Mexico, and then surviving as an immigrant in East LA. When she gave her life to Jesus five years ago, she became a walking testimony. Loretta does not go one day without praying, worshipping God, and reading her Bible. She is always loving someone in need, or sharing her faith. It is so fun to ask her, "So how was your day?" She always has a testimony to share. She is either praying for a co-worker, visiting a friend in the hospital, standing up for someone who is getting picked on, or hearing a powerful word from God for someone. Almost every day!

She walks through her day looking for God moments. She looks for ways to care for people and obey Jesus. During these years of following Jesus, she has experienced numerous medical and family problems. It would take pages to describe all the suffering she has gone through. As she says, if she didn't obey Jesus she might easily be an alcoholic, or simply have given up on life.

She will tell you that the pressures of her life are so great that if she doesn't "live for today" she won't make it. She leans on Jesus every day. As a result, instead of being in a very negative place, or her life being just like one of many in our community, she shines brightly.

She is an amazing leader and servant of God. More people go to her for counsel and prayer than anyone else in our church because they know that she has been through what they are going through, and they know that she has seen transformation and victory. Instead of being washed up or dried out, she is a walking inspiration. She expects to experience Jesus every day.

After the year of walking with my friend through OA, I began to be more consistent with my daily times with Jesus. I saw my deep need for His help, and I believed His instruction was for my good. I was caught up in His eternal perspective and became more consumed with just experiencing Him today. What a difference it has made in my life!

As we trust the eternal to Jesus' care and believe that the kingdom of God can come today, we are set up for an entirely new kind of life. In just one week, we may pray for people on multiple occasions, see God heal someone, reconcile tension in a relationship, step into multiple opportunities to be a servant, and persevere through purposeful suffering. All in just one week! We are not promised fireworks every day. Yet we are offered long-term transformation.

GOING FORWARD

IT IS IMPORTANT to have long-term goals and dreams, and it is crucial that we live with an eternal perspective. Yet it is so refreshing to realize that all God expects from us is to seek Him, obey Him, and trust Him today. We can't control anything except what is happening right now.

The faith-filled, joy-filled, transformed life of following Jesus means understanding and trusting in Jesus' eternal worldview, while also being consumed with finding Jesus today. Instead of being anxious about all the things that are not going right in your life, sit down and pour out your heart to God. Then focus on how you need to obey God today.

As you finish this book, sit down and come up with a new action plan. Ask God for His insights as you answer the questions at the end of this chapter. Saying yes to Jesus is saying yes to a great journey. One of the more tragic things that the American church has done is present Christianity as just a few big events: exciting at first, but soon a simple routine. But in reality, if you put your life into the hands of Jesus and commit to following His leadership, then you are choosing a lifelong transformative adventure. Getting out of bed every day is exciting!

The place we occupy now, in this lifetime, is not our true home; rather, heaven is our true home, and we must choose to journey towards heaven and our eternal treasure. If we say yes to this journey, we must understand that sin will always be our companion. There will be no rest from the fight against this great enemy until we meet God face to face. How we handle this fight on a daily basis characterizes who we are.

Jesus-followers thirst for transformation. As they continue in the journey, their passion continually increases—passion for overcoming the addictions of the flesh (our sinful nature), removing anything that dulls love and zeal for Jesus, and pleasing the heart of God. The simple things in our day—going to work, connecting with a stranger at the store, or coming home to an evening with family—are opportunities to live in the heart of Jesus, just as the big things are. Some days we will be overcome with sin. But just as the sun rises in the morning, breaking through the darkness, we too will rise the next day, running into the arms of our heavenly Father to find new strength to fight again.

Looking back at the end of our lives, we will be overwhelmed by the grace and mercy of Jesus. We will realize that Jesus not only persisted in leading us toward His commands, but He also never stopped giving us all that we needed to obey them. In the end, we will stand wide-eyed and open-mouthed at our new selves, shocked into silence over the grand transformation. There won't be an ounce of self-pride, but rather an overflowing fountain of worship of Jesus. Our transformed lives will be proof, once again, that He truly is the source of love, power, healing, wisdom, and new life.

Say yes to the journey. Trust Jesus. Live to obey Him TODAY.

QUESTIONS TO CONSIDER

1. How can you pursue more of God's love in daily prayer? Where will you pray? When will you pray?

2. What steps of courage will you take in representing Jesus to others? How can you better serve others as Jesus did? What sins do you need to confess and repent from in order to better display Jesus to others?

3. Who are you going to share your new action plan
   with? Who will keep you accountable?

A 30-WEEK TRANSFORMATION DISCIPLESHIP PLAN

THE JOURNEY OF TRANSFORMATION begins with a choice to trust our lives to Jesus and obey Him. Following Jesus is not just about adopting a new philosophy or seeking after new feelings. Central to following Jesus is a new relationship. Christianity is unique in that it is rooted in the person of Jesus. As we seek transformation in our lives, we are seeking a life characterized by the Holy Spirit living inside of us, helping us think, feel, and act like Jesus.

There is no magic prayer or special meeting that instantly does this work. It is developed through a journey of discipleship. It is not a journey we do on our own. We are to be discipled by others and we are to disciple others. We are to walk this journey in community with our spiritual family. The following is a thirty-week discipleship journey through the Sermon on the Mount. The goal is to be immersed in Jesus' words and to obey them before we move onto the next teaching. There is no fancy curriculum or special formula, just simple questions to help us engage with the teaching of Jesus.

WORDS TO WALK BY

Timeframe and structure

I HAVE FOUND that thirty weeks (between seven and eight months) is a good timeframe to commit to a discipleship relationship. At the end of thirty weeks, both the discipler and the disciple can evaluate whether or not to continue the discipling relationship. If you feel it would be better to start with a four- or six-month commitment, start there. Many people balk at thirty weeks, fearing it is too long. Jesus took three years to develop His disciples! The quick weekend boot camp or one-month class is not how life transformation happens. My best discipling relationships have all lasted more than a year. Trust Jesus and His methods, and sink into a real commitment.

I have structured this plan so that the entire Sermon on the Mount is broken into fifteen sections. Each section has only a few questions. The point is not to debate over every word. The point is to understand the main point and then obey (Matthew 7:24-29)! You should meet with your partner every week, though it is only every other week that you will move on to a new section. During the off weeks, talk about how obedience of that section of teaching is going, and encourage each other to continue practicing obedience for another week before moving on to the new section. By slowing down and putting more emphasis on action, we honor Jesus' teaching.

Feel free to be flexible with the structure. If you are in a good flow, it may make sense to move to the next section more quickly. If there is hunger and obedience, keep going! This study is simply an anchor for the discipleship relationship, something to refer to when things get difficult. Your relationship should be about more than these meetings and reflections on the Sermon on the Mount. The heart of a discipleship relationship is showing, and receiving, Jesus' love. (See 2 Timothy 1:1-7, which reveals the deep love Paul had for Timothy.) Learn about their life and become a great friend. Then regularly reflect with them on the areas God is revealing to them as needing growth. We want to both affirm their strengths and help in the areas where they are weak.

The importance of life together

ANOTHER ASPECT of the discipleship process is living life together. Jesus lived with His disciples for three years, eating, traveling, and working together. Most of what people learn about Jesus gets "caught" more than taught. In a discipleship relationship, we choose to overlap lives during these thirty weeks so that we can better model Jesus' teachings. Doing life together is the most challenging part of discipleship, especially for those of us who have families or crazy work schedules. Here are three practical ways that we can live life together in the midst of busyness:

✓ Schedule one road trip within these thirty weeks. This could be a fun trip, or it could be mission-oriented, where you serve another church in a different area together. Make sure your families are included and pick a cool spot that is not too far away, but far enough to warrant the title, "road trip." In the same way in which a weekend conference is better than three months of Sunday services, a road trip is a great way to bond, learn about each other, and develop a level of trust that will make the discipleship journey more authentic. The hope is that everyone will be able to let down their guard, allowing others, and Jesus, in.

✓ Schedule one or two Saturdays when you do errands together. Do your laundry together, wash your car, make your Target run, clean your house, etc. Whatever you both need to get done for that week, get it done together. That's it—just join each other in a regular Saturday of life.

✓ Invite each other to family functions. When there is a family birthday party or special dinner, invite each other (and the immediate family, if that applies). Don't worry about them seeing your family warts; it will only deepen your influence and help them open up about their family warts. Maggie and I have had multiple people we were discipling live with us for a year or more. It gets a little messy at times, but isn't all of life? It gives us a chance to model how we are bringing Jesus into our family, and also running to Jesus for help in the transformation of our family.

Before committing to a discipleship relationship

BEFORE YOU LAUNCH into this study together, begin with a short description of the general framework for discipleship I mentioned earlier: transformation in our relationship with God, our relationship with our Christian family/the church, and our relationship to the world.[52]

Within these three foundational relationships are numerous specific ways that God will challenge us to grow. For example, in our relationship with God, we will work on a daily time of prayer, how to study and center our lives on the Bible, how to hear God's voice, how to receive His Holy Spirit for power, etc. In our relationship with other Christians, we will work on serving and strengthening our church, discipling other people, understanding our spiritual gifts, etc. In our relationship with the world, we will work on how to share our faith with those who don't understand Jesus, how to enter into real relationships with the poor, how to break down walls that exist between different ethnic groups, how to serve our neighborhoods, etc. There are many ways God challenges us to grow through the course of discipleship, but in general, this particular discipleship model centers upon these three relationships.

Before you begin a discipling relationship with this plan, be sure that the person you are discipling has decided to follow Jesus and understands the central role of Jesus' work on the cross in order that they might be forgiven of their sins and have eternal life. Be sure they understand that the only way to fully obey the teachings of Jesus is through the grace of Jesus and the power of the Holy Spirit. Walking through the Sermon on the Mount should not be purely an exercise of will. You will need to return continually to this grace and power that is freely given. Having this basic framework and foundation is helpful, as it provides accurate expectations for the journey.

The first practical thing you want to help them with is their prayer life and daily time with Jesus. Help them set a realistic goal based on where they are at that moment. Throughout the discipleship journey, continue to dialogue about challenges that arise as they spend time with Jesus every day. Try to hold the tension between unlimited grace in failure, and the need to continue striving after time with God. As mentioned above, walking through the Sermon on the Mount will convict us that we need to spend time with Jesus in order to obey!

It is crucial that Jesus becomes their lifelong discipler, not any one person. Work on how to listen to God and hear His voice through prayer and Scripture.[53] Help them through their fears and insecurities of hearing God. Encourage them to tell you whatever they hear or see in their times of listening prayer. Be vulnerable with them about times you have heard wrong, and encourage them with the times God has spoken clearly. Celebrate when it is clear they have heard God!

Who do we invite into a discipling relationship? This is an important decision. In general, we look for people who are:

✓ Faithful: They are demonstrating hunger for God and a desire to grow.

✓ Available: They have space in their lives to commit to you and the discipleship journey.

✓ Teachable: They desire and are open to input, knowing they can't grow on their own.

As you consider someone to disciple, ask a trusted friend or leader to process the decision with you before you offer an invitation. Finally, make sure to seek the Lord's guidance before you give an invitation. Jesus prayed all night before choosing the twelve disciples (Luke 6:12-16).

What to do when the road is bumpy

EVEN WITH A good process, we may sometimes enter into a discipling relationship that stalls. The person we are discipling is not available, or unwilling to grow. In this case, seek out counsel, and then have a time of evaluation with the person you are discipling. Explain that this is not something that should be forced, and if they want to back out of it, that is fine. Maybe down the road it can start again.

As leaders, we can get frustrated when the person we are discipling does not seem to be growing spiritually. If they are not growing because they are resistant to Jesus' leadership in their lives, it may be time to end the relationship. However, if they are genuinely hungry and giving their best effort, but simply have deeply entrenched habits or struggles, then we need to endure with them and serve them in a slower process. In this case, wait until the end of the thirty-week commitment to evaluate if you should continue. I have had a couple of discipling relationships that have lasted three years because growth was slow, and now those people are discipling others! We can't put our personal worth or value in the speed of their growth. We endure with others just as Jesus endures with us.

Final thoughts

ONE OF THE GREAT lessons I have learned through living and walking with my friends of East LA is that life is messy. Life with Jesus is messy. Life with Jesus is not predictable, controllable, flashy, or "professional." But life with Jesus is full of healing and transformation.

We live in a culture that demands instant change, and follows superficial, professional leadership. Jesus leads us away from that, into a raw, difficult, enduring journey of carving away the sin cancer from our lives so that we can show the world something real. Don't expect to arrive anytime soon. But do expect to be loved till the very end. As a seventy-year-old transformed disciple said when asked the secret of her love and authority, "Stick with Jesus, dear. Stick with Jesus."

Don't let the long process take you away from Jesus in search of a new fad or new trend. Keep going back to what is true. Keep going back to the one who created you, to the one who has walked through all the suffering you endure and who will sit lovingly with you in all of your trials. Stick with Jesus.

Listen and obey. Learn and obey. Love and obey. Stick with Jesus and you will shine as lights in a very dark world.

---

[52] Mark 12:28-31, Luke 10:25-37, Acts 2:42-47, Galatians 6:2.
[53] Consider the story of Peter and Cornelius in Acts 10 as a biblical example of how listening prayer is central in the obedience process.

SERMON ON THE MOUNT STUDY GUIDE

Matthew 5:1-16

"Now when Jesus saw the crowds, he went up on a mountainside and sat down. His disciples came to him, and he began to teach them.

He said:
'Blessed are the poor in spirit,
for theirs is the kingdom of heaven.
Blessed are those who mourn,
for they will be comforted.
Blessed are the meek,
for they will inherit the earth.
Blessed are those who hunger and
thirst for righteousness,
for they will be filled.
Blessed are the merciful,
for they will be shown mercy.
Blessed are the pure in heart,

for they will see God.
Blessed are the peacemakers,
    for they will be called children of God.
Blessed are those who are persecuted because of righteousness,
    for theirs is the kingdom of heaven.

Blessed are you when people insult you, persecute you and falsely say all kinds of evil against you because of me. Rejoice and be glad, because great is your reward in heaven, for in the same way they persecuted the prophets who were before you.'"

"You are the salt of the earth. But if the salt loses its saltiness, how can it be made salty again? It is no longer good for anything, except to be thrown out and trampled underfoot.

"You are the light of the world. A town built on a hill cannot be hidden. 15 Neither do people light a lamp and put it under a bowl. Instead they put it on its stand, and it gives light to everyone in the house. 16 In the same way, let your light shine before others, that they may see your good deeds and glorify your Father in heaven."

REFLECTION QUESTIONS

- How do we understand the sharp differences between God's desire for how we should live and the world's expectations of how we should live?

- Do our lives appear to be as sharply different when compared to those around us who do not walk with Jesus?

- What do we need to focus on in our lives in order to start being better salt and light to others, so that they might see God in us?

Matthew 5:17-26

"Do not think that I have come to abolish the Law or the Prophets; I have not come to abolish them but to fulfill them. For truly I tell you, until heaven and earth disappear, not the smallest letter, not the least stroke of a pen, will by any means disappear from the Law until everything is accomplished. Therefore anyone who sets aside one of the least of these commands and teaches others accordingly will be called least in the kingdom of heaven, but whoever practices and teaches these commands will be called great in the kingdom of heaven. For I tell you that unless your righteousness surpasses that of the Pharisees and the teachers of the law, you will certainly not enter the kingdom of heaven.

"You have heard that it was said to the people long ago, 'You shall not murder, and anyone who murders will be subject to judgment.' But I tell you that anyone who is angry with a brother or sister will be subject to judgment. Again, anyone who says to a brother or sister, 'Raca,' is answerable to the court. And anyone who says, 'You fool!' will be in danger of the fire of hell.

"Therefore, if you are offering your gift at the altar and there remember that your brother or sister has something against you, leave your gift there in front of the altar. First go and be reconciled to them; then come and offer your gift.

"Settle matters quickly with your adversary who is taking you to court. Do it while you are still together on the way, or your adversary may hand you over to the judge, and the judge may hand you over to the officer, and you may be thrown into prison. Truly I tell you, you will not get out until you have paid the last penny.

REFLECTION QUESTIONS

- How does this teaching speak to your life about any areas of anger you might have toward someone?

- This passage shows we can't worship God if we have issues and problems with other people. Why is that?

- Is there someone you need to reconcile with in your life, among family, friends, co-workers, or someone in your spiritual or church community?

Matthew 5:27-30

"You have heard that it was said, 'You shall not commit adultery.' But I tell you that anyone who looks at a woman lustfully has already committed adultery with her in his heart. If your right eye causes you to stumble, gouge it out and throw it away. It is better for you to lose one part of your body than for your whole body to be thrown into hell. And if your right hand causes you to stumble, cut it off and throw it away. It is better for you to lose one part of your body than for your whole body to go into hell."

REFLECTION QUESTIONS

- How does God describe sin here?

- What do you think of this idea that thinking about a woman lustfully (including pornography) is the same as sleeping with her?

- What can we cut out of our lives to fight sexual temptation and keep it from growing?

Matthew 5:31-37

"It has been said, 'Anyone who divorces his wife must give her a certificate of divorce.' But I tell you that anyone who divorces his wife, except for sexual immorality, makes her the victim of adultery, and anyone who marries a divorced woman commits adultery. Again, you have heard that it was said to the people long ago, 'Do not break your oath, but fulfill to the Lord the vows you have made.' But I tell you, do not swear an oath at all: either by heaven, for it is God's throne; or by the earth, for it is his footstool; or by Jerusalem, for it is the city of the Great King. And do not swear by your head, for you cannot make even one hair white or black. All you need to say is simply 'Yes' or 'No'; anything beyond this comes from the evil one."

REFLECTION QUESTIONS

- Why would God care about whether we are true to our word?

- As you think about commitments you've made, what are specific reasons why you may fail to follow through on them?

- How can you work against those to become someone who is true to your word?

Matthew 5:38-48

"You have heard that it was said, 'Eye for eye, and tooth for tooth.' But I tell you, do not resist an evil person. If anyone slaps you on the right cheek, turn to them the other cheek also. And if anyone wants to sue you and take your shirt, hand over your coat as well. If anyone forces you to go one mile, go with them two miles. Give to the one who asks you, and do not turn away from the one who wants to borrow from you.

You have heard that it was said, 'Love your neighbor[i] and hate your enemy.' But I tell you, love your enemies and pray for those who persecute you, that you may be children of your Father in heaven. He causes his sun to rise on the evil and the good, and sends rain on the righteous and the unrighteous. If you love those who love you, what reward will you get? Are not even the tax collectors doing that? And if you greet only your own people, what are you doing more than others? Do not even pagans do that? Be perfect, therefore, as your heavenly Father is perfect."

REFLECTION QUESTIONS

- What does God think about revenge?

- How can we love our enemies but not be abused by them?

- How does loving your enemy make you "perfect" in the same way God our Father is perfect?

Matthew 6:1-4

""Be careful not to practice your righteousness in front of others to be seen by them. If you do, you will have no reward from your Father in heaven.

So when you give to the needy, do not announce it with trumpets, as the hypocrites do in the synagogues and on the streets, to be honored by others. Truly I tell you, they have received their reward in full. But when you give to the needy, do not let your left hand know what your right hand is doing, so that your giving may be in secret. Then your Father, who sees what is done in secret, will reward you.

REFLECTION QUESTIONS

- Who are the needy in your world? Why are they needy?

- How can we love any of the needy around us in ways that are genuine, while not seeking praise from others for any of the giving we might do?

- What can we do this week to care in secret for any needy we see, trusting God's seeing and reward?

Matthew 6:5-14

""And when you pray, do not be like the hypocrites, for they love to pray standing in the synagogues and on the street corners to be seen by others. Truly I tell you, they have received their reward in full. But when you pray, go into your room, close the door and pray to your Father, who is unseen. Then your Father, who sees what is done in secret, will reward you. And when you pray, do not keep on babbling like pagans, for they think they will be heard because of their many words. Do not be like them, for your Father knows what you need before you ask him.

> This, then, is how you should pray:
> Our Father in heaven,
> hallowed be your name,
> your kingdom come,
> your will be done,
>   on earth as it is in heaven.
> Give us today our daily bread.
> And forgive us our debts,
>   as we also have forgiven our debtors.
> And lead us not into temptation,
>   but deliver us from the evil one.

For if you forgive other people when they sin against you, your heavenly Father will also forgive you. But if you do not forgive others their sins, your Father will not forgive your sins.

REFLECTION QUESTIONS

- Why must we have not only have a public spirituality (church service, life group, conferences, our discipleship time, etc.), but also a private relationship with God?

- How are your personal and private times with Jesus?

- What clear and simple element of the Lord's Prayer (including prayers of praise, need, forgiveness, protection, and deliverance) do we each need to focus on right now?

Matthew 6:16-18

"When you fast, do not look somber as the hypocrites do, for they disfigure their faces to show others they are fasting. Truly I tell you, they have received their reward in full. But when you fast, put oil on your head and wash your face, so that it will not be obvious to others that you are fasting, but only to your Father, who is unseen; and your Father, who sees what is done in secret, will reward you."

REFLECTION QUESTIONS

- What do you think about fasting?

- We are promised blessings and rewards for fasting—if we fast for the right reasons. What are right motivations or wrong motivations for fasting?

- How can we fast this week, perhaps together with others in our church or spiritual community, to break sin in our lives and get more of Jesus?

Matthew 6:19-24

"Do not store up for yourselves treasures on earth, where moths and vermin destroy, and where thieves break in and steal. But store up for yourselves treasures in heaven, where moths and vermin do not destroy, and where thieves do not break in and steal. For where your treasure is, there your heart will be also.

The eye is the lamp of the body. If your eyes are healthy, your whole body will be full of light. But if your eyes are unhealthy, your whole body will be full of darkness. If then the light within you is darkness, how great is that darkness!

No one can serve two masters. Either you will hate the one and love the other, or you will be devoted to the one and despise the other. You cannot serve both God and money."

REFLECTION QUESTIONS

- What does it mean to serve money as a master with authority over your life?

- What does it mean to use our money or any kind of treasure we have for eternal things rather than earthly things?

- How do you feel about money management in your life right now?

Matthew 6:25-34

"Therefore I tell you, do not worry about your life, what you will eat or drink; or about your body, what you will wear. Is not life more than food, and the body more than clothes? Look at the birds of the air; they do not sow or reap or store away in barns, and yet your heavenly Father feeds them. Are you not much more valuable than they? Can any one of you by worrying add a single hour to your life?

And why do you worry about clothes? See how the flowers of the field grow. They do not labor or spin. Yet I tell you that not even Solomon in all his splendor was dressed like one of these. If that is how God clothes the grass of the field, which is here today and tomorrow is thrown into the fire, will he not much more clothe you—you of little faith? So do not worry, saying, 'What shall we eat?' or 'What shall we drink?' or 'What shall we wear?' For the pagans run after all these things, and your heavenly Father knows that you need them. But seek first his kingdom and his righteousness, and all these things will be given to you as well. Therefore do not worry about tomorrow, for tomorrow will worry about itself. Each day has enough trouble of its own.

REFLECTION QUESTIONS

- How often do you worry about having enough money for your needs?

- How would joy and freedom increase in your life if you truly believed and followed this command?

- What does seeking God's kingdom first in your life mean to you right now?

Matthew 7:1-6

"Do not judge, or you too will be judged. For in the same way you judge others, you will be judged, and with the measure you use, it will be measured to you.

"Why do you look at the speck of sawdust in your brother's eye and pay no attention to the plank in your own eye? How can you say to your brother, 'Let me take the speck out of your eye,' when all the time there is a plank in your own eye? You hypocrite, first take the plank out of your own eye, and then you will see clearly to remove the speck from your brother's eye.

Do not give dogs what is sacred; do not throw your pearls to pigs. If you do, they may trample them under their feet, and turn and tear you to pieces."

REFLECTION QUESTIONS

- Why might God judge or measure us in the same way we judge or measure others?

- Why is it important to protect what is holy?

- How can we help each other live in humility throughout this week?

Matthew 7:7-12

"Ask and it will be given to you; seek and you will find; knock and the door will be opened to you. For everyone who asks receives; the one who seeks finds; and to the one who knocks, the door will be opened.

Which of you, if your son asks for bread, will give him a stone? Or if he asks for a fish, will give him a snake? If you, then, though you are evil, know how to give good gifts to your children, how much more will your Father in heaven give good gifts to those who ask him!"

REFLECTION QUESTIONS

- What does it mean to ask, to seek, or to knock, in our relationship with God and as we are part of His kingdom in this world?

- Do you believe God is a great Father and loves to give you good gifts?

- What specifically do you want to ask for this week, every day, to place your trust in God as a good Father, and a giver of good gifts?

Matthew 7:12-20

"So in everything, do to others what you would have them do to you, for this sums up the Law and the Prophets. Enter through the narrow gate. For wide is the gate and broad is the road that leads to destruction, and many enter through it. But small is the gate and narrow the road that leads to life, and only a few find it.

Watch out for false prophets. They come to you in sheep's clothing, but inwardly they are ferocious wolves. By their fruit you will recognize them. Do people pick grapes from thornbushes, or figs from thistles? Likewise, every good tree bears good fruit, but a bad tree bears bad fruit. A good tree cannot bear bad fruit, and a bad tree cannot bear good fruit. Every tree that does not bear good fruit is cut down and thrown into the fire. Thus, by their fruit you will recognize them."

REFLECTION QUESTIONS

- How does the golden rule, "Do unto others as you would have them do unto you," help us hold the whole teaching of God in our hearts?

- How does the path following Jesus seem narrow to you, and how does taking the easy path lead to destruction?

- Where do you see good fruit or bad fruit coming from your own life?

Matthew 7:21-23

"Not everyone who says to me, 'Lord, Lord,' will enter the kingdom of heaven, but only the one who does the will of my Father who is in heaven. Many will say to me on that day, 'Lord, Lord, did we not prophesy in your name and in your name drive out demons and in your name perform many miracles?' Then I will tell them plainly, 'I never knew you. Away from me, you evildoers!'"

REFLECTION QUESTIONS

- What is the difference between calling on Jesus as Lord and doing the will of Jesus' Father in heaven?

- What is the difference between doing great works in Jesus' name, including even prophesying and casting out demons, and being known by Jesus?

- What is the most important part of this for you to obey in your life right now?

Matthew 7:24-29

"Therefore everyone who hears these words of mine and puts them into practice is like a wise man who built his house on the rock. The rain came down, the streams rose, and the winds blew and beat against that house; yet it did not fall, because it had its foundation on the rock. But everyone who hears these words of mine and does not put them into practice is like a foolish man who built his house on sand. The rain came down, the streams rose, and the winds blew and beat against that house, and it fell with a great crash."

When Jesus had finished saying these things, the crowds were amazed at his teaching, because he taught as one who had authority, and not as their teachers of the law.

REFLECTION QUESTIONS

- If you do what Jesus commands, how does that make you like a wise person who builds their house on house rock rather than on sand?

- What kind of "storms" hit our lives that threaten to destroy our homes, our lives, and our foundations?

- Why and how will your house stay strong even in the worst storm if you follow Jesus commands with action rather than only intellectual understanding or positive emotion?

Matthew 28:18-20

[After Jesus' death on the cross and his resurrection from the dead]

"Then Jesus came to them and said, "All authority in heaven and on earth has been given to me. Therefore go and make disciples of all nations, baptizing them in the name of the Father and of the Son and of the Holy Spirit, and teaching them to obey everything I have commanded you. And surely I am with you always, to the very end of the age."

REFLECTION QUESTIONS

- What does it mean that all authority in heaven and earth has been given to Jesus?

- What specific commands are found in Jesus' last words to His disciples here?

- What does it mean to you that Jesus will be with you always?

BIBLIOGRAPHY

Arterburn, Stephen. *Every Man's Battle: Winning the War on Sexual Temptation One Victory at a Time*. Colorado Springs: Waterbrook, 2009.

Butterfield, Rosaria Champagne. *The Secret Thoughts of an Unlikely Convert: An English Professor's Journey into the Christian Faith*. Pittsburgh: Crown & Covenant, 2012.

Chapman, Gary. *Anger: Handling a Powerful Emotion in a Healthy Way*. Chicago: Northfield, 2007.

Coleman, Robert E. *The Master Plan of Evangelism*. Grand Rapids: Baker, 1963.

Engdahl, Derek W. *The Great Chasm: How to Stop Our Wealth from Separating Us from the Poor and God*. Pomona: Servant Partners Press, 2015.

Ethridge, Shannon. *Every Woman's Battle: Discovering God's Plan for Sexual and Emotional Fulfillment*. Colorado Springs: Waterbrook, 2009.

Foster, Richard J. *Celebration of Discipline: The Path to Spiritual Growth*. New York: HarperCollins, 1978.

Hagner, Donald A. *Word Biblical Commentary: Matthew 1-13*. Dallas: Word Books, 1993.

Herber, Robert. *Changing the World through Discipleship: Vision, Practical Steps, and Tools for Every Believer to Fulfill Jesus' Great Commission*. San Diego: All People's Church, 2011.

Johnson, Jan. *When Food Is Your Best Friend and Worst Enemy*. San Francisco: HarperCollins, 1993.

King, Martin Luther Jr. *Strength to Love*. Minneapolis: Fortress, 2010.

Lawson, Josh. *Realign: Finding God's Purpose for Your Money*. Brentwood: Clear Day, 2014.

Nysewander, Mark. *The Fasting Key: How You Can Unlock Doors to Spiritual Blessing*. Grand Rapids: Servant Publications, 2003.

Piper, John. *A Hunger for God: Desiring God through Fasting and Prayer*. Wheaton, IL: Crossway, 1997.

Piper, John. *Desiring God: Meditations of a Christian Hedonist*. Sisters: Multnomah, 1986.

Ryle, J. C. *Holiness: Its Nature, Hindrances, Difficulties, and Roots*. Durham: Evangelical Press, 1979.

Seibert, Jimmy. *Passion and Purpose: Believing the Church Can Still Change the World*. Brentwood, TN: Clear Day, 2014.

Willard, Dallas. *The Divine Conspiracy: Rediscovering Our Hidden Life in God*. San Francisco: HarperCollins, 1988.

Willard, Dallas. *The Spirit of the Disciplines: Understanding How God Changes Lives*. New York: HarperCollins, 1988.

ABOUT THE AUTHOR

CHRIS HAS LIVED for almost 20 years in the urban poor communities of Los Angeles. Most of these years have been in East LA, where he, his wife Maggie, and their three children have planted roots. His children are proud participants in the Los Angeles public school system, where they have learned both Spanish and Mandarin through LAUSD's Dual Immersion program. Chris has helped plant two churches and also founded In the City, a non-profit dedicated to educational support in his neighborhood. He is currently preparing for the next church plant by mentoring a new generation of leaders from his community through the Discipleship School that he leads. He loves to coach people into greater relationship to Jesus, greater character, and greater leadership.

Chris is available in a limited capacity to speak with interested groups. To arrange please contact Servant Partners Press at 626.398.1010 or email *press@servantpartners.org*.

CPSIA information can be obtained
at www.ICGtesting.com
Printed in the USA
FSOW01n0836280117
30030FS